John Edgar

The Homeric Hymns

John Edgar

The Homeric Hymns

ISBN/EAN: 9783744768580

Printed in Europe, USA, Canada, Australia, Japan

Cover: Foto ©Thomas Meinert / pixelio.de

More available books at **www.hansebooks.com**

THE
HOMERIC HYMNS

TRANSLATED INTO ENGLISH PROSE

BY

JOHN EDGAR, B.A. (Oxon.); M.A. (Glasgow)

FORMERLY SNELL EXHIBITIONER OF BALLIOL COLLEGE, NOW CLASSICAL
MASTER IN THE ROYAL HIGH SCHOOL, EDINBURGH; TRANSLATOR
OF AESCHINES IN CTESIPHONTEM

EDINBURGH
JAMES THIN
55 SOUTH BRIDGE

1891

Who, fretted by the haste of fevered life,
Harks to the prisoned voice of murmurous shell,
In fancy wanders by the grey sea swell,
And rests on quiet shore—mid city strife.
Great boon! if brine-crisp air be far away,
And the blue infinite of sky be hid,
And streets monotonous be round him thrid
By care-worn mortals lacking time to stay.

So in the shell of old Homeric lays,
We hear hymned echoes from the world's prime,
When gods were shepherding on hill and plain;
And though the simple faith, the glad surprise
Of gods revealed, the glamour of old time
Be far away, our hearts beat fresh again.

INTRODUCTION.

INTRODUCTION.

THE following pages contain a translation into English prose of the old Epic preludes and lays known as the Homeric Hymns. The scholars of England have imitated the great ancient critics of Alexandria in treating the collection of poems with unmerited coldness. The Iliad and the Odyssey are such bright suns in the firmament of poesy, that the lesser lights of these Hymns have not been so conspicuous in the world of literary scholarship as their worth and interest deserve. They are ancient, but not ancient enough; and our scholars, having assured themselves that they were Post-Homeric, have left the work of editing and annotating them almost entirely to the Germans. Yet the poems, more especially the longer ones, contain much that is beautiful and interesting to the classical student, and afford a fertile field for the exercise of scholarly taste and critical ability. The motto which heads Dr Gemoll's preface is an apt one:—

"ὁ μὲν θέλων μάχεσθαι
πάρεστι γὰρ μαχέσθω."

There are certainly difficulties and obscurities

enough in the text to tempt any scholar who is seeking for new worlds to conquer. The poems have an interest also to the student of Mythology and the History of Religion. They come midway between Homer and the Tragedians; and though we find in the collection Hymns to deities who were unknown to Homer, the simple and rude ideas of the early Greeks still prevail. The mystic and philosophic developments of later times are only traced in one or two of the more recent poems. Therefore, as Grote says, "they do to a certain extent continue the same stream of feeling, and the same mythical tone and colouring as the Iliad and the Odyssey, manifesting but little evidence of Egyptian, Asiatic, or Thracian adulterations."

Their Date.

As Homer—the eponymous founder of the Epic, the author or authors of the primary Iliad and Odyssey—marked the close of the early minstrel or ballad period, so also he marked the beginning of a new Epic period, and gave rise to a new order of minstrels. For he was succeeded by a long line of bards and reciters, first perhaps known as Homeridae, and afterwards, when public recitations of Homer became more and more a recognized part of public festivals, as Rhapsodists. The later Rhapsodists were not composers—it was enough for them to recite the poems of Homer, and make them vivid and impressive to the people of Greece; but many of the earlier were themselves poets, and that too of no mean order. How far they had a share in adding to and cementing the original Iliad and Odyssey we cannot say, but it is certain that they often recited their own compositions, and sometimes even passed them off as the offspring of the Homeric Muse. The Homeric Hymns are a collection of original preludes and Epic lays recited by these Homeric Rhapsodists.

They are not the work of any one author or age. It is improbable that any of them was composed earlier than the first Olympiad—B.C. 776, though Müller was of opinion that this collection contained specimens belonging to every century between Homer and the Persian wars.

Of the longer Hymns, that to Aphrodité is probably the oldest, and that to Hermes the latest. Many even of the shorter poems contain some phrase or reference to guide us in fixing a probable date-limit. The great majority belong to the period between B.C. 700 and B.C. 450; but for a full discussion of the age of the individual poems I must refer the reader to the notes of Baumeister and Gemoll.

If we accept the now commonly received doctrine that the Iliad and the Odyssey had received their present complete form by B.C. 800, then there is no doubt at all that the whole of the Hymns are Post-Homeric. But Professor Jebb, in his book on Homer (p. 155), says, "The bulk of the Homeric poems must be older than B.C. 800, although some particular additions to them are later;" and again (p. 173), in discussing the age of the Odyssey, "It cannot be shown, then, that Kirchhoff has gone too low in assigning circ. 660 B.C. as the date of the second enlargement." If we take advantage of these admissions of modern scholarship, it is at least within the bounds of probability that the poets who composed the Hymn to Aphrodité and the Delian Apollo had some share in giving to the Iliad and the Odyssey their present form, and are not without a fair claim to be sheltered under the great name of Homer. That many authors at different times must have had a share in the composition of these Hymns is shown by their great internal differences of style and language, and also by the fact that some of them are evidently copies and imitations of others (*vide* Gemoll, p. 103). One of them indeed is a literal transcription from Hesiod, and another undoubtedly owes its origin to the Boeotian School. Most of the important Hymns contain some hint to guide us in fixing the place where they were recited; and their geographical range, like their date of composition, covers a wide area. Thus the Hymn to the Delian Apollo was doubtless recited at Delos, and that to the Pythian Apollo at Delphi. The Hymn to Ceres belongs to the Panathenaic Festival. The Hymns to Dionysus (vii. and xxvi.) were apparently recited at the Brauronia, and Hymn ix. (To Diana) at the temple of the goddess at Colophon.

Their Name and Origin.

There has been a good deal of discussion as to the name given to this collection of poems. The word Hymn suggests to us a sacred lyric or song in honour of the Deity. And ὕμνος, from which the word is derived, carried with it in classical Greek a similar connotation. Now the poems under consideration are not lyrics, and their name is used in a more general sense, though they all contain some invocation to a god. Both by nature and history they differ from lyric and choral song, and claim near kinship with the Epic poems of the Homeric School. The word ὕμνος, being derived from the stem ὑφ, to weave, would have a root meaning of "web." And from this comes the general meaning "song" or "lay." Hermann denies that the ancients have any such usage of the word, but later scholars have brought forward several quotations to prove that he was wrong. For example, Od. viii. 429 "ἀοιδῆς ὕμνον ἀκούων." Hesiod, "*Works and Days*," 662; *Theogony*, 101. It is probable, therefore, that the word "ὕμνος" as applied to these poems, is to be understood in this general sense of "song" or "lay." And the formula so often used at the end of these poems, "μεταβήσομαι ἄλλον ἐς ὕμνον," will strengthen the probability for us, if we remember that the poems were being recited at some contest of Homeric Rhapsodists.

From the frequent occurrence of such phrases as πῶς τ' ἄρα σ' ὑμνήσω in poems narrating some incident in the life of a god or hero, the word ὕμνος acquired by association its later and more specific meaning of a song in honour of a god. Thus the Scholiast to Soph. Electra defines it "ὕμνος κυρίως ἡ εἰς θεὸν ᾠδή."

Strange to say the word προοίμιον, which some consider the more correct title for these poems, has quite the opposite history. Its original application was to Hymns in honour of Apollo (Thucy., iii. 104), who, as patron of song, was generally first invoked in the poetical contests at the Festivals. From that special use it became generalised and was employed in the sense of prelude.

Mure, in his "History of Greek Literature," vol. ii., divides the Hellenic Hymns into three classes— Mythical, Mystical, and Philosophical. It is to the first or Mythical class that the Hymns in this collection almost entirely belong, as dealing with the genealogy, actions, and attributes of the Hellenic Gods. The Mystical and Philosophical classes are represented by the Orphic collection, to which the Hymn to Ares (viii.) ought also to be added. These Homeric Hymns again naturally divide themselves into—1st, A great many short poems; 2nd, Six or seven of considerable length and distinctly Epic in character.

To have a clear understanding of the nature and origin of these Hymns, we must keep before us the fact that the ancient minstrels or ballad singers, who sang to the accompaniment of the lyre at the feasts in princely houses, gave place from the time of Homer downwards to the professional Reciter or Rhapsodist. The Epic metre was unsuited to a musical accompaniment, the word ἀείδειν came to mean "recite," and for a period the lyre was retained only as a tribute to conventional usage. A staff was the later symbol of the minstrel's office.

To the great Festivals held in various parts of Greece the Rhapsodists gathered. Down to the sixth century they probably had complete freedom of choice, and recited poems composed by themselves as well as the notable Epics. Afterwards, as the living editions of Homer, they made known throughout the country the great poems which told the story of the gods and heroes. Prizes were given to the most successful or the most popular, and in several of the Hymns before us the Rhapsodist, who still calls himself a minstrel, prays to the god for honour and success. Now it was the prevalent custom that before the recital proper of the Epic Rhapsody began, an invocation or prelude to some god was delivered by the Rhapsodists. It was like the opening psalm which so often in our own day initiates a religious service or a public ceremony. These exordia or preludes were doubtless in most cases composed by the Rhapsodist himself to suit his own taste and the requirements of the special Festival. The twenty-eight smaller poems in this collection seem then, with only one or two exceptions, to be specimens of these religious preludes. The nature and general drift of the poems supports this, and there are two phrases which establish it beyond a doubt.

H. xxxi. 18. "ἐκ σέο δ᾽ ἀρξάμενος κλήσω μερόπων γένος ἀνδρῶν ἡμιθέων."

H. xxxii. 18. "σεο δ᾽ ἀρξάμενος κλέα φώτων ᾄσομαι ἡμιθέων, ὧν κλειουσ᾽ ἔργματ᾽ ἀοιδοί."

The *Locus Classicus*, which proves generally that it was customary at these Epic contests to recite an opening Hymn to the gods, is Plutarch de Musicâ, c. 4. "τὰ πρὸς τοὺς θεούς, ὡς βούλονται, ἀφοσιωσάμενοι ἐξέβαινον εὐθὺς ἐπί τε τὴν Ὁμήρου καὶ τῶν ἄλλων ποίησιν."

To the same effect writes the Scholiast to Pindar. Nem. ii. "ὅλως γὰρ οὗτοι εἰς τὸν Δία προοιμιασάμενοι τουντεῦθεν ἤδη τῆς ἐποποιίας ἥπτοντο."

It is just possible, however, that some of these short poems served not as opening but as closing Hymns in the rhapsodic recitals. The phrase "πρῶτον καὶ ὕστατον ἀείδειν" shows that the god invoked at the beginning would also be honoured at the end. And at the close of several Hymns, *e.g.*, xxi., we find the formula καὶ σὺ οὕτω χαῖρε, without any transition verse to suggest that other poems were to follow. The assumption, therefore, is a legitimate one, that these may have been end-poems, marking the completion of a series of Rhapsodies.

The longer Hymns.

But what are we to say about the six longer Hymns—viz., To the Delian Apollo, the Pythian Apollo, Hermes, Aphrodité, Ceres, and Dionysus? Even an uncritical mind must see that these are too long, if not also too secular in spirit, to be religious opening Hymns. The most natural, as well as the most generally accepted belief, is that they were not introductions to rhapsodies, but rhapsodies themselves, making up along with other similar poems or extracts from Homer a Rhapsodic series. They may, of course, have been the inaugural poems in their respective series. The Hymns to Apollo would doubtless take the first place in accordance with general usage, and the closing verse of the Hymn to Aphrodité, "σεῦ δ' ἐγὼ ἀρξάμενος, &c.," makes it certain that this poem also occupied the same position. The formulae at the end of the Hymns to Hermes and Demeter show at least that other poems were still to be recited by the same rhapsodist.

Mure thinks that the Delian and Pythian Hymns "may have originally succeeded each other in the customary order of celebration, the one as prooemium, descriptive of Apollo's birth, the other recording the spread of his influence," and that they may have got run together into one by a natural confusion of the editors. But though the original editors did indeed confound them into one, it could hardly have been for this reason. The Pythian Hymn is a later production, and in its structure bears so curious a resemblance to the other that it must have been an imitation. Moreover, it is almost certain that the one was recited at Delos, and the other at Delphi.

These larger Hymns, then, are Epic Lays, having as their central theme some action of a deity, round which other incidents or characteristics group themselves, but never in such proportions as to mar the poetic unity of the poem. They are closely allied in character with the Song of the minstrel Demodocus in the Odyssey, which might be called a Homeric Hymn to Hephaestus if the usual formulae of invocation were added. These Hymns, then, may be said to carry on the tradition of the earlier Balladists, whose songs led up to and were absorbed in the great Epics of Homer.

Introduction. 19

Why attributed to Homer?

The conventional usage of antiquity was to attribute these Hymns to Homer. But the name, doubtless, was meant in many cases to stand not for the person of the poet, but his school. Sometimes they are spoken of as " εἰς Ὅμηρον ἀναφερόμενοι," and " ἐπιγραφόμενοι Ὁμήρῳ." There is no doubt, however, that Thucydides believed in Homer's authorship of the Delian Hymn to Apollo. In Book III., 104, while speaking of Delos he makes some quotations from that poem which he calls a προοίμιον. The passage containing the reference to Homer's authorship is as follows : " ὅτι δὲ καὶ μουσικῆς ἀγὼν ἦν καὶ ἀγωνιούμενοι ἐφοίτων, ἐν τοῖσδε αὖ δηλοῖ, ἅ ἐστὶν ἐκ τοῦ αὐτοῦ προοιμίου· τὸν γὰρ Δηλιακὸν χορὸν τῶν γυναικῶν ὑμνήσας ἐτελεύτα τοῦ ἐπαίνου ἐς τάδε τὰ ἔπη, ἐν οἷς καὶ ἑαυτοῦ ἐπεμνήσθη." The testimony of Thucydides is always weighty, and his words at any rate prove that even in the best educated circles of Athens, Homer was considered the author of the Delian Hymn. But Thucydides was not a professional critic, and in his day literary criticism was but in its infancy, though the standard of poetic taste was high. And it is fairly certain, that though it is not impossible that the author of this Hymn may have had some share in the latest additions to the Iliad or the Odyssey, he must have flourished at a later period than the real composers of these Epics. For not to mention points of diction, we may recall the fact pointed out by Strabo, that Samos to Homer always meant Samothrace; that Delos is only once mentioned in the Odyssey, and had evidently not yet risen to fame; and further, the word πρυτανεύειν in i. 68 suggests the conclusion of Baumeister, that the Greek colonies of Asia Minor had by this time been founded.

The testimony of Thucydides, however, strengthens the other evidence which goes to prove that the author could not have been Cinaethus of Chius, if he flourished about the 69th Olympiad. A poem composed only some eighty years before his own time would hardly have been attributed to Homer by the great historian. We are only justified in inferring from the famous closing lines of the Delian Hymn, that its author was a blind man, who lived in Chios, wandered about reciting his poetry from city to city, claimed for himself persuasive influence, and for his poems immortal renown: and finally lived at a period when Delos had become famous from its connection with Apollo, and gathered crowds of Ionians to its Festivals. In addition to Thucydides, many other classical authors of considerable antiquity ascribe the Hymns to Homer: *e.g.*, Herodotus in Life of Homer, Suidas, Pausanias, Diodorus. But in most cases they merely represent the conventional opinion, and their evidence goes for little in face of the results of later criticism.

Since, then, the Hymns were not composed by Homer, as being of later date than the first Olympiad, when the Iliad and the Odyssey seem to have been practically as complete as we now have them, how did they come to be attributed to him?

Various answers have been given to the question. Some who trace the influence of the Orphic School in many of the poems, assert that poets of that school to win honour for their own productions ascribed them to Homer; others that they were well known as having been recited at the contests of Homeric Rhapsodists, and were thus connected with Homer's name. Groddeck, Ilgen, and others consider that their Epic style caused them to be attributed to the founder of Epic poetry; and Wolf thought that, like so many other anonymous poems, they were fathered on the name which stood out most prominently. To a similar effect Mure says: "The deference paid to Homer by his own immediate successors amounted to so close a spirit of imitation as to have caused the principal Epic productions of the ensuing age, amid the uncertainty as to their real authors, to be classed in popular usage as inferior productions of his own muse." Bergk and Gemoll hold that the real reason is to be found in the closing verses of the Hymn to the Delian Apollo. There the author calls himself a blind singer, and according to the popular legend Homer was blind. Gemoll points out the possibility that the legend about the blindness was itself derived from the Hymn, and that the reputation of its authorship may be older than the legend. But he finds a further proof in the bard's prophecy that his poems will be immortal, for he holds that to a Greek, immortal verse would at once suggest Homer. It is evident that these reasons are not inconsistent with each other, and that where so many explanations can be given, the result could not have been very difficult to bring about.

The Collection.

The collection of Hymns before us is of considerable antiquity, and though we cannot with accuracy fix its date, it seems to have existed in the third century B.C., and to have been ascribed to Homer. We find testimony for this in various references, quotations, and imitations. Antigonus Carystius quotes the Hymn to Hermes when discussing the number of strings on the ancient lyre. Diodorus, i. 15, &c., praises "Homer in the Hymns." The statement of Pausanias that the Orphic Hymns for beauty rank next to the Hymns of Homer, seems to imply a knowledge of some collection like that before us. It is probable also that

Callimachus and Theocritus knew the Hymns, for they have written several conscious or unconscious imitations. And the same may be said about Apollonius Rhodius, on the strength of the great resemblance between Book IV., 877, &c., to a passage in the Hymn to Demeter.

It is curious, in view of the many references to the Hymns by important classical writers from Thucydides downwards, that the Alexandrine scholars, the leading ancient authorities on Homeric matters, should have so completely overlooked and neglected them. Their silence regarding them is so complete that the only scholia which can be quoted to show that they knew them at all, go no further back than the age of Augustus, and therefore do not come near the dates of their greatest scholars, Zenodotus and Aristarchus.

Wolf thought that they intentionally ignored them as being non-Homeric. And the very results of their scholarly researches prove that they did not consider the Hymns to illustrate Homeric usage. For example, they assert that Homer in his poems makes no mention of himself, and their statements about Homeric geography show that they took no account at all of the use in the Hymns of Samos, Europa, and Peloponnesus. Whatever was the reason for their silence, it is difficult to believe that it was complete ignorance of the poems.

Whoever the person was that brought together in one volume these Hymns, he must have had an imperfect acquaintance with Homeric poetry, or he would not have admitted the Hymn to Ares (viii.), a poem with all the characteristics of the Orphic School. There are others of the Hymns which have but a doubtful claim to their position, and the twenty-fifth is a mere patchwork of Hesiodic verses.

Baumeister thinks that after a period of flitting existence from mouth to mouth of the rhapsodists, the poems were committed to writing, and were finally collected by some librarian. The condition of the text makes it clear that this was done not with the critical skill and loving care of a scholar anxious to retain their original beauty, but with careless haste by a man of inferior education. A great deal has been done for the text by German editors. It still, however, leaves much to be desired, and we hope that some good English edition will be published before long. The need is great.

The text used in preparing this translation was that of Augustus Baumeister (Trubner, Leipsig, 1860). Where I have departed from his reading, the one preferred is given in a footnote. I have consulted the editions and annotations of Ilgen and Hermann, but have derived most assistance from the notes and introductory essays of Baumeister and Dr Albert Gemoll. The edition of Dr Gemoll (Trubner, Leipsig, 1886) is in every respect a valuable one, embodying as it does within its pages the most recent results of German scholarship.

EDINBURGH, 1890.

TRANSLATION.

CONTENTS

		PAGES
I. To the Delian Apollo	. . .	29-35
II. To the Pythian Apollo	. . .	36-50
III. To Hermes	. . . . .	50-73
IV. To Aphrodité	. . . .	73-84
V. To Demeter	. . . .	84-103
VI. To Aphrodité	. . . .	103-104
VII. To Dionysus	. . . .	104-106
VIII. To Ares	. . . . .	106
IX. To Artemis	. . . .	107
X. To Aphrodité	. . . .	107
XI. To Athené	. . . .	108
XII. To Hera	. . . . .	108
XIII. To Demeter	. . . .	109
XIV. To the Mother of the Gods	. .	109
XV. To Heracles	. . . .	109
XVI. To Asclepius	. . . .	110
XVII. To the Dioscuri	. . . .	110
XVIII. To Hermes	. . . .	110
XIX. To Pan	. . . . .	111-113
XX. To Hephaestus	. . . .	113
XXI. To Apollo	. . . .	114
XXII. To Poseidon	. . . .	114
XXIII. To Zeus	. . . . .	114
XXIV. To Hestia	. . . .	115
XXV. To the Muses and Apollo	. .	115
XXVI. To Dionysus	. . . .	115
XXVII. To Artemis	. . . .	116
XXVIII. To Athené	. . . .	117
XXIX. To Hestia	. . . .	118
XXX. To the Mother of All	. . .	119
XXXI. To Helios	. . . .	120
XXXII. To Selené	. . . .	121
XXXIII. To the Dioscuri	. . . .	122
XXXIV. To Dionysus (a fragment)	. .	123

THE HOMERIC HYMNS.

I.

TO THE DELIAN APOLLO.

I SHALL remember and forget not Apollo, the Far Darter, at whose step down the hall of Zeus the gods tremble. Yea, they all start up from their seats when he cometh nigh, holding bent his shining bow. Leto alone abideth by Zeus the Thunderer; she slackeneth his bow-string and shutteth his quiver, and from his stalwart shoulders taketh his bow with her hands and hangeth it on a golden peg against the pillar of his sire. Therewithal she leads him to his seat. And his father welcomes his dear son, giving him nectar in a golden cup. Then first do the other gods seat them there. And queenly Leto is glad withal in that she hath borne as a son the mighty Archer. (Hail, O Leto! Blessed in bearing glorious children —Apollo the King, and Artemis the Huntress— thy son in rugged Delos, thy daughter in Ortygia— crouching against the long bent of the Cynthian hill near a palm tree by the streams of Inopus.) How shall I praise thee fully, praised as thou art in many a hymn? To thee, O Phoebus, above all have been allotted the fields (νομοί) of song, both on the calf-rearing mainland, and from isle to isle. Thou hast had delight in all rocks, in the steep crags of tall mountains, in rivers hurrying seaward, in shingles sloping to the tide, and harbours of the sea.

Shall I sing how Leto bore thee first, a joy to men —as she lay on Mount Cynthus, in the rugged isle of sea-washed Delos, on whose either side the dark wave drifted landward before the shrill breezes? There wert thou born, and thou art Lord of all the folk within the borders of Crete and Athens, the isle Aegina, and Euboea, famous on the sea, Piresian Aegae, and sea-bound Peparethus, Thracian Athos, and the peaks of Pelion, Thracian Samos and the shadowy heights of Ida, Scyros and Phocaea and the steep hill of Autocané, fair-built Imbros, and inhospitable Lemnos, goodly Lesbos, the seat of Aeolian Macar, and Chios, richest isle that nestles in the sea, craggy Mimas and the peaks of Corycus, bright Claros and the steep hill of Aesagea, watery Samos, the lofty heights of Mycale, Miletus and Cos, the city of the Meropes, and towering Cnidus, and windy Carpathus, and Naxos, and Paros, and rocky Rhenaea. Thus widely did Leto fare in travail with the Far Darter if peradventure any of the lands would be willing to give a home to her son. But they trembled sore and were afraid, and no land dared to welcome Phoebus, not even the most fertile, till queenly Leto set foot upon Delos, and questioned her with winged words: "O Delos, would that thou wert willing to be the home of my son, Phoebus Apollo, and to let raise him a rich temple. None other god will ever choose thee, nor honour thee, nor wilt thou ever, methinketh, be rich in cattle nor in sheep, nor wilt thou bear corn, or grow countless trees. But if thou possessest a temple of Apollo the Far Darter, all men will gather hither to thee, bringing hecatombs, and thou wilt ever have plenteous incense . . . from alien hands as thy soil is infertile."

Thus she spoke, and Delos was glad, and said in reply : " O Leto, glorious daughter of mighty Corus, gladly should I welcome the birth of the Far Darting Prince, for verily I have a sorry name among men, and hereby should I wax high in honour. But I tremble, Leto, at this rumour. I shall not hide it from thee. Exceeding haughty, they say, will Apollo be, and high lordship will he hold over immortal gods and mortal folk on the rich cornlands. Therefore I sorely dread in mind and heart, lest whenas first he beholdeth the sunlight, he may scorn mine island, for rocky is my soil, and spurning me with his foot may drive me under the depths of the sea. Then for ever a great wave will wash over my head in its strength. And to some other land which delighteth him will he go to fashion him a temple and leafy groves. And on me the sea-urchins will make them their nests and the black seals their lairs in safety from lack of men. But if thou wert minded, Goddess, to swear me a solemn oath that here first he will build a beautiful temple to be a shrine for mortals . . . then among all mankind, since his fame is wide."

Thus Delos spake. And Leto swore the great solemn oath of the gods: "Bear me witness, O Earth and wide Heaven above, and downward flowing waters of Styx, the greatest and dreadest oath among the blessed gods. Verily here there shall be for ever a fragrant altar and garth of Apollo, and thee will he honour above all."

When she had sworn and ended the oath, Delos greatly rejoiced at the coming of the Far Darting King. But for nine days and nights was Leto pierced with desperate pangs. With her were all the worthiest goddesses, Dione and Rheia, and Ichnaean Themis, and moaning Amphitrité, and the other immortal ones save white-armed Hera (for she sat in the halls of Zeus the Cloud Gatherer). Eilithuia alone, the Helper in travail, had not heard the tidings thereof. She was sitting on the top of Olympus, under the golden clouds by the planning of white-armed Hera, who was detaining her in jealousy, whenas fair-tressed Leto was soon to bring forth her stalwart blameless son.

But the goddesses sent forth Iris from the fair-set island to bring Eilithuia, and promised her a great golden necklace, braided with amber, nine cubits long. Their bidding was to call her aloof from white-armed Hera, lest even then Hera by her words might turn her from her going. When swift, wind-footed Iris had heard their bidding, she hasted on apace and quickly accomplished all the distance. On reaching the home of the gods, steep Olympus, she straightway called Eilithuia to the door from out the hall, and spake to her winged words, all just as the Olympian goddesses had bidden. And she persuaded the heart of Eilithuia in her breast. And they fared forth afoot, moving like timorous wild doves.

When Eilithuia, Helper of Travail, had come to Delos, then did labour take hold of Leto, and she was fain to be delivered. Round a palm tree she threw her arms, and pressed her knees on the soft sward. The earth smiled beneath her. So the child sprang forth to the light, and the goddesses raised the birth-shout. Then, O Phoebus, Sung of Men, did the goddesses bathe thee in fair water clean and pure, and wrap thee in swaddling clothes, white, dainty, and newly woven, and round thee put a golden girdle. His mother suckled not Apollo of the Golden Sword, but Themis hanselled his immortal lips with nectar and sweet ambrosia. And Leto was glad because she was the mother of a brave son, The Archer. But as soon, O Phoebus, as thou hadst eaten the food divine, no longer did the golden girdle hold thee for thy panting, nor the bands confine thee, but all the ends were loosed. And straightway to the immortal ones did Phoebus Apollo say, "Give me a dear lyre and a curving bow, and to men shall I declare the true counsel of Zeus." With these words he began to walk over the broad-wayed earth—Phoebus, the Unshorn, the Far Darter. And all the goddesses marvelled. The whole of Delos bloomed in gold, as when a hill-top is laden with tree-blossoms, beholding the child of Zeus and Leto, and in joyance that the god had chosen her for his home before the isles and the mainland, and loved her more dearly.

All by thyself, O King of the Silver Bow, Far Darting Apollo, didst thou now fare over craggy Cynthus, anon wander among the islands and the folk. Many are thy temples and wooded groves. Dear to thee are all the heights and sharp forelands of tall mountains and rivers flowing seaward, but chiefly dost thou delight thy heart in Delos, where the long-robed Ionians gather in thine honour with their children and chaste wives. They give thee joy, celebrating thee with boxing and dancing and song when they hold their Festival. Whoso meeteth the Ionians at their gatherings will say that they are immortal and ageless. For he will see the beauty of them all, and delight his soul with gazing on their men and their fair-girdled women, their swift ships and their many possessions. And withal there is this great marvel, the fame of which will never perish—to wit, the damsels of Delos, hand-maidens of the Far Darter, who, when first they have sung of Apollo, make mention of Leto and Artemis the Huntress, chanting a hymn about the men and women of old, and charm the kindreds of the folk. And they wot how to imitate the tones and dance-step* of all men. Each would fancy that himself were singing, so well is their fair song woven together.

But now gracious be Apollo and Artemis! Farewell, ye maidens all! Remember me even in days to come, when any wandering stranger of earth-born men wendeth hither and asketh, "Maidens! who is the sweetest to you of the minstrels faring hither, and in whom take ye most delight?" Do ye one and all make the friendly answer, "A blind man, who dwelleth in rocky Chios. His songs will be the best even in days to come." And I shall bear your fame, far as I travel over the earth to fair-builded cities. And men will believe me, since sooth it is. But I shall not cease singing of Far Darting Apollo of the Silver Bow, whom Leto the Fair Tressed bore.

* Or "musical accompaniment."

II.

TO THE PYTHIAN APOLLO.

O King, thine are Lycia, and lovely Maeonia, and Miletus, the fair city by the sea, and thou too art the mighty Lord of wave-washed Delos.

The Son of glorious Leto fareth to rocky Pytho, playing on his bent lyre—his divine raiment fragrant with incense, and sweet is the tone of his lyre beneath the golden plectrum. Thence from earth to Olympus, swift as thought, he hieth to the assembly of the other gods at the hall of Zeus. Straightway the immortals bethink them of harp and song. And all the Muses in joint refrain chant with sweet voices of the divine gifts of the gods and the sorrows of men which by the dealings of the deathless gods they bear, living reckless and helpless; nor can they find a cure for death or defence against old age. But the fair-tressed Graces and blithe Seasons; Harmony, and Hebé, and Aphrodité, Daughter of Zeus, hold each the other's hand at the wrist and dance. Among them danceth one, neither unfair nor unstately—nay, very tall to look upon, and lovely in form— Artemis the Huntress, sister to Apollo. And amid them sport Ares and the keen-eyed Slayer of Argos. But Phoebus Apollo playeth the lyre.

High and graceful is his step. Round him flasheth the gleam of twinkling feet and of fair-woven robe. And they are glad in their great hearts—Leto of the Golden Tresses, and Zeus the Counsellor—to see their dear son sporting amid the immortal gods.

How shall I praise thee fully, praised as thou art in many a hymn? Shall I sing of thee among suitors and love-making—how thou didst go a-wooing the damsel Azanis, with god-like Ischus, Elation's son, the lover of horses? or Phorbas, son of Triopes, or Amarynthus? or how along with Leucippus and the wife of Leucippus . . . thyself afoot, he on the chariot . . . ?

Or how at first in quest of an oracle for men thou didst fare to earth, O Far Darting Apollo? To Pieria first thou didst descend from Olympus, and didst go to Lacmus and Emathea, and Enienae, and through Perrhaebia. Soon thou camest to Iolcus, and didst set foot upon Cenaeum in Euboea, famed for ships. And thou didst stand on the Plain of Lelantum. But it pleased not thy heart to raise a temple there and wooded grove. Thence crossing Euripus, O Far Darter, thou faredst up the rich green fell, and therefrom didst speedily reach Mycalessus on thy way and meadowy Teumessus. And thou camest to the forest-clad site of Thebes, for not yet in sacred Thebes did any one of mortals dwell. Nor were there yet roads or paths along the wheat-bearing plain of Thebes. All was forest. Thence thou didst hie forward, Far Darting Apollo, and come to Onchestus, the splendid grove of Poseidon. There the new-broke colt takes fresh breath though spent with dragging the beautiful chariot. And his driver, good though he be, leaps to the ground from the car and foots it on the road. The colts meanwhile freed from guidance, rattle along the empty chariot. If they lead it within the wooded grove, their masters let them feed, and leave the chariot tilted. Such was the olden rite. And the drivers pray to King (Poseidon), and the providence of the god now guardeth the car. Thence didst thou hie forward, Far Darting Apollo, and get thee next to the fair-flowing Cephissus, which from Lilaea poureth forth its fair stream. Crossing this, and passing turretted Ocalea, thou didst thereafter come to grassy Haliartus. And thou didst set foot upon Telphussa. This peaceful spot did please thee whereon to raise a temple and wooded grove.

Hard by Telphussa thou didst stand, and speak this word to her: "O Telphussa, here do I purpose to build a beautiful temple as an oracle for men who will ever come hither to consult me, bringing perfect hecatombs, the dwellers both in rich Peloponnesus, and in Europe and the sea-girt isles. To them, one and all, shall I rede true dooms giving responses in my rich temple.

Thus spoke Phoebus Apollo, and marked out fully the foundations—broad and very long. But Telphussa at the sight was wroth at heart, and thus addressed him: "O Phoebus, King, Far Darter! one word shall I set in thine heart. Inasmuch as thou art purposing to build here a beautiful temple to be a shrine for men who will ever be bringing thee hither perfect hecatombs, one thing would I tell thee, and do thou lay it up in thine heart. Ever will the clatter of swift horses annoy thee, and the watering of mules at my sacred springs. And some of mortals will wish rather to gaze on the goodly chariots and hear the clatter of nimble steeds, than (to see) thy great temple and the many treasures within it.

"But if thou wilt reck my rede—though thou art stronger, O King, and mightier than I, and sovran is thy power—build for thyself in Crissa among the foldings of Parnassus. There will neither fair chariots shake, nor swift steeds clatter around thy well-builded altar; but in peace will the famous kindreds of men bring their gifts to Ia-paeon, and glad at heart wilt thou receive the goodly sacrifices of the neighbouring folk."

With these words she persuaded the mind of the Far Darter to the end that she, Telphussa, alone might have glory in the land, and not the Far Darter.

Thence didst thou fare forward, Far-casting

Apollo, and come to the city of the Phlegyes, an overweening folk, who recking nought of Zeus, dwelt in the land within a fair glen near the Lake of Cephissus. Therefrom apace thou didst quickly advance to the uplands. And thou gattest thee to Crissa, beneath snowy Parnassus, a slope that faced the west. Above it hangs a cliff, and beneath run the shaggy hollows of the glen. There Phoebus Apollo, the King, trysted him to build a beautiful temple, and spake these words: "Here do I purpose to build a beautiful temple as an oracle for men who will ever come hither to consult me, bringing perfect hecatombs—the dwellers both in rich Peloponnesus, and in Europe and the sea-girt isles. To them, one and all, shall I rede true dooms giving responses in my rich temple."

Thus spake Phoebus Apollo, and marked out fully the foundations—broad and very long. And upon them Trophonius and Agamedes, sons of Erginus, dear to the immortal gods, built an inner shrine of stone, and round it countless tribes of men raised a temple of polished stones, to be sung of for ever. Near by is a clear flowing spring, where the King, the son of Zeus, with his mighty bow slew a dragoness, stark and huge, a monster fierce, which was working much harm to the people in the land, both to the folk themselves, and to their long-shanked sheep—for it was a cruel pest.

Erstwhile did the dragoness receive from golden-throned Hera the dire and terrible Typhaon, and rear him a curse to men. To him did Hera give birth because of her anger at Father Zeus, whenas Cronides had begotten from his head glorious Athené. Straightway was queenly Hera wroth, and spake thus among the assembled gods. "Hear from me, ye gods and goddesses all, how Zeus, the Cloud Gatherer, beginneth to dishonour me though he hath made me his dutiful wife. Even now he hath without mine aid begotten the bright-eyed Athené, who excelleth among all the blessed immortals. Whereas mine own son Hephaestus, the halt of foot, is the meanest among all the gods,* whom I myself erst raised in my hands and hurled down, casting him into the broad sea. But Thetis, the daughter of Nereus, the Silver-footed, received him and nursed him among her sisters. Would that other favour she had done to the immortal gods! Cruel and crafty Zeus! what new device is this? How hast thou dared of thyself to give birth to bright-eyed Athené? Could not I have brought her forth? Yea, and thine entirely hath she been called among the immortals who keep wide heaven. Beware now, that I devise not for thee some future ill. Yea, I shall forthwith contrive that a son be born to me who shall excel among the immortal gods, and that without dishonouring thy sacred

---

* v. 139. Read with Gemoll, "ὅν τε ποτ' αὐτή," and remove asterisks.

bed or mine own. And I shall not go to thy couch, but abiding far aloof from thee I shall consort with the immortal gods." Thus having spoken she moved away from the gods with angry heart. Then forthwith prayed Ox-eyed Queenly Hera, and striking the ground with down-turned hand, uttered this word: "Hear me now, O Earth and broad Heaven above, and ye Titans divine who dwell beneath the ground in vast Tartarus, and from whom spring gods and men. List to me now all of you, and grant me a son without the aid of Zeus, in nought inferior to him in strength. Nay, stronger may he be, as far as Zeus the Far-seer is stronger than Cronos."

With these words she struck the ground with the palm of her hand. And Earth the life-giver moved. Hera at the sight rejoiced in her heart, for she weened that her prayer was fulfilling. Thenceforth for a full year she came not once to the bed of Zeus the Counsellor, nor to his beautiful seat as aforetime (when she sat thereon and planned shrewd counsels), but Ox-eyed Queenly Hera abode in her temples where many pray, and took delight in her sacrifices. Now when the days and nights of the revolving year were being accomplished and the seasons came round, she brought forth a child like neither unto gods nor men—the dire and terrible Typhaon —a curse for mortals. Forthwith the Ox-eyed

Queenly Hera took him up and gave him to the dragoness, thereby joining plague to plague. And the dragoness received him: and many were the woes she wrought among the famous kindreds of men.

Whosoever met her, on him she would bring the day of doom, until the King, Far Darting Apollo, let loose upon her his arrow in his strength. Then rent with grievous pangs she lay panting sorely and rolling over the ground. A weird, awful sound arose. Hither and thither through the wood full many times she rolled, and left her murderous soul in death. Over her Phoebus Apollo invoked this curse: "There now rot upon the fruitful ground. Thou at least shalt no longer live to be a woeful scourge to the folk who eating the fruit of the fertile land shall bring hither perfect hecatombs. In nowise from ruthless death shall Typhoeus nor the hateful Chimaera shield thee, but the swart Earth and Hyperion the Slayer shall rot thee where thou liest."

Thus did he speak his curse. But darkness shrouded her eyes. And the sacred might of Helios rotted her where she lay. Hence now is she called Pytho. Him they hight the Pythian King, for there where she lay the strength of the fleet Helios rotted the monster.

Then did Phoebus Apollo wot in his heart why the fair-flowing Fountain had bewrayed him.

Wroth against Telphussa he set out, and speedily was come. Hard by her he took his stand, and thus addressed her: . "Telphussa, it was not fated that by deceiving my heart thou shouldest keep this goodly land and pour forth thy fair waters. Here my fame too shall flourish, not thine alone."

The King, the Far Darting Apollo, spake and pushed a rock over her stony outlet, and hid her streams, and withal he made for himself an altar in the wooded grove close by the fair-flowing spring. There all men name him in prayer Telphousian King, because he hath dishonoured the streams of sacred Telphussa. Then did Apollo in his heart bethink himself what folk he should fetch as priests, to minister in rocky Pytho, to offer sacrifices, and tell forth the dooms of Phoebus Apollo of the Golden Sword, whatso he should say of weird ·from the laurel tree in the dells of Parnassus. As he pondered thereon, he espied on the wine-dark sea a swift barque. Aboard her were many good mariners—Cretans from Cnossus, the city of Minos, who to the King . . .

For barter and wealth were they voyaging in their dark ship to sandy Pylos and the folk of Pylus. But Phoebus Apollo fared to meet them. In form like a dolphin he leapt upon the swift ship in the sea, and lay on deck a huge and terrible monster. Not one of the crew guessed in his heart or wotted what he was. . . .

He shook the barque on every side and strained her timbers. And the crew sat still on the ship in terror. Not even did they undo the tackling in their dark vessel, nor haul up the sail of their purple prow, but as first they had set their sail, so did they voyage on. And the fresh south wind behind sped on the swift ship. First they passed Malea, and skirting the Laconian land came to Helos, a town by the sea, and Taenarus, the demesne of Helios, who gladdeneth men, where the long-fleeced sheep of King Helios ever feed, and possess the pleasant land. There were the crew fain to put in, and go ashore to mark the great marvel and behold with their eyes whether the monster would abide on the deck of the hollow ship or leap again into the teeming gulf of the sea. But their trim vessel obeyed not the rudder, but fared on her way of herself beyond fertile Peloponnesus. And the King, Far Darting Apollo, sped her lightly before the breeze. Coursing on her journey she came to Arené, and fair Argyphea, and Thryum, ford of the Alpheus, and well-builded Aepu, and sandy Pylos, and the folk of Pylos. On she fared past Krouni, and Chalcis and Dymé, and divine Elis where the Epeans hold sway. When she was nearing Pherae, exulting in the wind of Zeus, from out the clouds was revealed to them the tall peak of Ithaca and Dulichium, and Samé. and wooded Zacynthus.

But when now she had passed clear beyond Peloponnesus, off Crissa was soon revealed the wide gulf which bounds the fertile Peloponnese all along. And there arose a fresh strong west wind by the will of Zeus, rushing stiffly through the sky, that the ship might swiftly finish her course over the briny sea. Back they sailed towards the East and the Sun : their pilot was King Apollo, Son of Zeus. So they came to far-seen, vine-clad Crissa, into the harbour, and their seafaring vessel grazed the shingle. Then the King, Far Darting Apollo, leaped from the ship like a meteor at midday, and many sparks flew from him, and the gleam flashed into the sky, and through the precious Tripods he entered his shrine. There did he kindle his flame and display his shafts, and the light covered the whole of Crissa. The wives of the Crissaeans and their fair-girdled daughters raised their wail at the flashing of Phoebus, for great fear laid hold on all. Thence swift as thought, back again to the ship he leaped and sped, looking like unto a lusty and strong man in his prime, with his hair covering his broad shoulders. In winged words he addressed the crew : "Strangers, who are ye? whence sail ye the watery ways? Have ye been voyaging for traffic or at random, like pirates over the sea, who risk their life as rovers and bring ill to strangers? Why sit ye thus downcast, and get ye not ashore, nor do up the tackling of your dark ship? It is the way with toiling mariners when so in their dark ship they come ashore from the main, sated with labour, that forthwith a longing for sweet food taketh hold of their hearts." Thus he spake and set courage in their hearts. And to him the captain of the Cretans made answer, and said: "O stranger, inasmuch as thou art in nowise like unto mortal man, either in stature or face, but to the immortal gods. . . . Health and great joy be thine, and may the gods grant thee blessings. Pray, tell me this truly, that I may know for sooth. What people? what land is this? what folk live here? We were minded for another land as we sailed over the great sea, for Pylos from Crete, wherefrom we claim to spring. But now hither have we come with our ship by no will of ours (fain for our return, by other route and other ways), but one of the immortals brought us hither in our despite."

To them in answer spake Apollo, the Far Darter: "Strangers, who aforetime have sojourned in wooded Cnossus, no more now will ye return again each of you to his goodly city, his fair homestead, and dear wife. Here will ye keep my rich temple honoured among many folk. The Son of Zeus am I; I am hight Apollo. You have I brought hither over the great sea waste, purposing no ill, but here shall ye keep my rich temple which all men highly esteem, and ye shall know the counsels of the gods, by whose pleasure ye shall ever be honoured through all time. Come, speed ye to obey my bidding. First loose the ropes and lower the sails, then haul the swift ship ashore take out your cargo and the good ship's tackling, and build an altar on the shore of the sea. Thereon kindle a fire, and sprinkle in sacrifice withal the white meal. Then stand ye about the altar and make your prayer. Whereas at first on the misty sea, in dolphin shape, I leapt upon your swift ship, do ye pray to me as Delphinius, and my altar itself will ever be the Delphian altar, and will be seen afar. Thereafter do ye dine by the swift dark ship, and pour libations to the Blessed Gods, who hold Olympus. And when ye have driven away the desire of sweet food, come with me chanting the Paean, till ye reach the demesne where ye shall keep my rich temple." Thus spake Apollo, and the men were fain to listen and obey. First they loosened the ropes and lowered the sails, and letting down the mast by the forestays, they brought it to the crutch. Then the sailors disembarked on the shore of the sea, and from the water hauled on to the land their swift ship high upon the shingle, laying large blocks underneath. And they built an altar on the sea-beach, and kindling a fire sprinkled upon it white grain. Withal they prayed, as he bade them, standing about the altar. Thereafter they took their meal by the swift dark ship, and made libations to the Blessed Gods who hold Olympus. But when they had driven away the desire of food and drink, they started on the way. King Apollo, the Son of Zeus went before them, with noble and lofty stride, his lyre in his hands, playing sweetly. The Cretans followed him to Pytho, dancing and chanting Io-Paean, after the manner of the Paeans of the Cretans, whose breasts the divine Muse hath inspired with melodious song. With feet unwearied they drew nigh the hill, and quickly were come to Parnassus, and the goodly demesne where they were to dwell honoured of many folk. Apollo led the way and showed them his wealthy shrine and rich temple, whereat the spirit was stirred within their dear breasts. And the captain of the Cretans enquired of him, and said: "O King, since thou hast led us far from friends and dear fatherland—so hath it been pleasing to thy heart—we bid thee tell us how we are even now to live. This fair land neither beareth vines, nor is goodly with meadows that we should fare well thereon, and withal minister unto men." To them with a smile, Apollo, the Son of Zeus, made answer: "Foolish mortals, and unhappy! who are fain at heart for cares, sore toils, and straits. Easy is the rede I shall speak and set in your hearts. Let every man of you with a knife in his right hand ever slaughter sheep. All of those which the famous kindreds of men bring to me shall be yours, an ample store. Do ye guard my temple, and welcome the kindreds of men as they gather hither, and above all, respect my purpose. But if there be any rashness of word or deed, or any presumption, such as is common to mortals, then other men shall be your leaders, by whom you will be held perforce in thraldom for ever. All is spoken. Do you keep it in your heart. Farewell to thee now, O Son of Zeus and Leto. But I shall remember thee and another lay."

III.

TO HERMES.

Sing, O Muse of Hermes, the Son of Zeus and Maia, Lord of Cyllené, and pastoral Arcadia, Herald of Heaven, and Bringer of Luck. Maia, the fair-haired damsel, the debonair bare him to the caresses of Zeus. From the gathering of the Blessed Gods she held aloof, abiding in a dusky cave, where at the dead of night that sweet slumber might be fettering white-armed Hera, Cronion wooed the fair-haired damsel without the ken of the deathless gods or mortal men. Now when the purpose of mighty Zeus was fulfilling (and her tenth moon stood in the sky, she brought a child to the light, and notable deeds were done). In that hour she gave birth to a son, subtle of wit and wile, a robber, a reiver of cattle, a captain of thieves, a prowler of the night, a pilferer at gates, who was ere long to make known fine doings among the immortal gods. (At dawn was he born, at mid-day he was playing on the lute, in the evening he stole the oxen of Far Darting Apollo, on that fourth day of the month whereon the Queenly Maia bore him.) And the child, when he had leapt from his mother's womb divine, did not long lie idling in the sacred cradle, but up he sprang and crossed the threshold of the lofty cave, seeking the oxen of Apollo. There he found a tortoise—a prize, a countless treasure. (Out of the tortoise, Hermes was first to fashion a minstrel.) He happed on it at the outer door as it waddled along, cropping the lush grass afront the cave. At sight thereof, the Luck-bringing Son of Zeus laughed and hailed it thus: "An omen of great luck for me! I flout thee not. Welcome! my beauty! my dancer! my feast-mate! Vision of gladness! Whence comest thou hither, my fair toy, my speckled shell, my tortoise of the hills? Surely I will bear thee home in my hands. A boon thou wilt be to me, and I shall not scorn thee. Yea, thou wilt do me highest service. ''Tis better to bide at home when there is danger abroad.' For while alive thou wilt be a charm against baneful witchery, and when dead thou wilt utter sweetest music." Thus he spake, and in his twain hands he raised it, and hied within the house with his fair treasure. Then he bent the mountain-tortoise back, and with chisel of grey steel gouged out its flesh. As when swift thought passes through the breast of a man, whom thronging anxieties harass; as when glances flash from the eyes, so swiftly did famous Hermes devise and do. He pierced holes in the shelly back of the tortoise, and cutting reed-stalks to the lengths, fixed them therein. Athwart these by his wit he stretched an oxhide and fitted on the horns; to the two horns withal he fixed the crossbar. Then he stretched him seven harmonic gut-strings. When he had fashioned with his fingers the beautiful instrument, he touched the chords one by one with a plectrum, and the lyre sounded clearly to his hand. And the god sang to its accompaniment a beautiful song, improvising as he sang, as gallants at their feasts bandy reckless jests. He told of Zeus, the Son of Cronos, and Maia, the fair-sandalled, how aforetime they dallied in wanton love, and the story of his own famous birth. He sang also of the hand-maids, and the glorious halls of the Nymph; of the tripods withal, and the strong caldrons in the house.

Of such things did he sing, but other were

the thoughts of his heart. He took the hollow lyre and laid it in his sacred cradle, then longing for flesh-meat he sprang forth from the odorous hall to survey, pondering in his mind a fell scheme, such as robbers ply in the dark nighttide.

Helios had sunk beneath the earth into Ocean with his chariot and his horses, when Hermes came running to the misty heights of Pieria, where the divine oxen of the Blessed Gods had their stalls, and grazed on the beautiful unmown meadows. From their herd did the Son of Maia, Far-gazing Argeiphontes, sunder off fifty lowing kine. From side to side he drave them, over the sandy ground, inverting their trail. Forgetting not the art of his cunning, he reversed their hoofprints—the front behind, the hinder in front—and himself fared again down the mountain. When he had cast his shoon into the sand of the sea, he plaited wondrous work beyond imagining and thought, weaving together tamarisk and myrtle twigs. Then roping together a sheaf of this sprouting wood, which he had plucked on Pieria, he tied it as light sandals under his unshod feet, leaves and all, to disguise his footmarks, and turned himself from side to side like one hurrying on a secret errand.* But an aged carle, who

* v. 86. Read δολιήν for δολίχην, ἀλλοτροπήσας for αὐτοπρεπής ὥς, as Baumeister suggests in his note.

was setting a rich vineyard floor, espied him as he was hurrying to the plain through grassy Onchestus. Him first the Son of glorious Maia addressed: "Verily, old Crook-back, digging there among the trees, thou wilt have wine in plenty when all these bear fruit. Have eyes, I bid thee, but see not; have ears, but hear not, and be silent, as long as no scathe is come to thine own."

With these words he chased forward the strong kine. Over many a misty fell, and through echoing glens and flowery plains the famous Hermes drave them. But his murky ally Divine Night was well-nigh ended, and Morn that calleth to toil was quickly dawning, when the brave Son of Zeus drave the broad-backed kine of Phoebus Apollo to the river Alpheius. Unwearied they reached the high-roofed byre and the troughs that edged the shining meadow. When he had there fed well the lowing kine with fodder, he first drove them all together within the byre, munching lotus and dewy clover; then he gathered a pile of faggots, and had resort to the art of fire. Lifting a fine laurel branch he barked it with his knife and fitted it to his hands, . . . and the warm smoke arose. And he took many dry brands fit for burning, and placed these in plenty upon it within a hollow of the ground. The flame shone out, darting afar its stream of wide-blazing light. While the might of famous Hephaestus kept the fire alit, he dragged out near it two lowing ambling kine, for his strength was great, and threw them both panting to the ground upon their backs. Then bending down he rolled them round, and, adding task to task, bored out their lives and cut off the rich fat meat. This he pierced with wooden spits, and roasted the flesh, the broad chine, and the dark blood pursed in the entrails all together. And he laid it down there upon the ground. But the skins he stretched out on a flinty rock, as even now in later times they are made enduring—a long time after, a countless time. Therewithal did merry Hermes drag the fat carcases upon a smooth reef, and set apart twelve portions by lot—to each god allotting the offering due. Then glorious Hermes longed for the rite of the flesh-feast, since the sweet savour distressed him, immortal though he was. Natheless his stout heart yielded not, even to his strong desire, to let it pass his sacred throat. But he placed the fat and the plenteous flesh in the high-roofed byre, and quickly piled them high to be a trophy of his recent theft.* And heaping up dry faggots he destroyed the heads and feet entire with the breath of flame. When the god had finished all in order, he cast his sandals into deep-eddying Alpheius, quenched

---

* v. 136. If τὰ δὲ is to be understood here after the τὰ μὲν in 134, translate "As to the fat, &c. . . . he placed some of it, &c. . . . the rest, after heaping up dry faggots, he burned entirely."

the embers, and covered with dust the dry ashes.

Anon at dawn he reached again the divine heights of Cyllene. None met him on the long journey either of blessed gods or mortal men; not even did dogs bark at him.

With bended head Luck-bringing Hermes, the Son of Zeus, entered the hall through the bolt-hole like a wind of autumn or a mist. (And straightening himself he reached the rich inner chamber of the cave with soft treading feet; no creaking of footsteps was on the floor.) Quickly was glorious Hermes come to his cradle. Wrapping the swaddling clothes about his shoulders, he lay like an infant, his hands playing with the coverlet over his knees, his beautiful lyre guarded at his left.

But the god escaped not the eyes of his goddess mother, and she addressed him thus: "On what errand, Trickster, and from whence farest thou thus in the night-tide, bedight in impudence? Erelong, meseemeth, thou wilt either pass forth through the porch with strong fetters bound about thy ribs at Apollo's hands, or by-and-bye be a vile robber in the glens."

To her Hermes made answer with cunning words: "Mother mine, why fearest thou thus for me, as for an infant, which knoweth but little mischief in its heart—a trembling creature, which feareth a mother's chidings. Verily I shall ply my shrewdest skill in counselling myself and thee unceasingly. Nor shall we twain of the immortal gods brook to remain here without gifts and prayers. Better far to hold converse for ever among immortals—rich, unstinted, laden with spoil, than sit at home in a dark cavern. As for honour, I too shall obtain like worship with Apollo. Albeit if my sire grant it not, mine aim shall be (I have the power) to become a robber chieftain.

"But if the son of famous Leto seek me out, methinks I shall outplan him with another, aye, a greater scheme. For I shall go to Pytho, and break open his great temple, wherefrom I shall plunder great store of goodly tripods, and caldrons and gold, abundance of flashing iron, and much raiment. And if thou hast a mind, thyself shall see it."

Thus were they addressing each other—the Son of Aegis-bearing Zeus and Queenly Maia. But Morning, daughter of Dawn, was rising from the deep-flowing ocean, bringing light to men, when Apollo came on his way to Onchestus, the beautiful grove sacred to the boisterous Earth-Shaker. There he found an aged carle, the hump-back, trimming by the wayside his vineyard hedge. To him the Son of glorious Leto first made speech: "Aged hedge-cutter of grassy Onchestus hither, am I faring in quest of cattle from Pieria—all the kine, the crook-horned kine from my herd. My black bull was wont to pasture aloof from the rest, and my keen-eyed dogs followed in the rear—four of them, clever as men, and one in heart. They were left—the dogs and the bull—and herein is marvel great, but the kine went away from their sweet grazing in the meadow just when the sun went down. Prithee tell me, ancient carle, if thou hast anywhere seen a man wending his way after my kine."

To him in reply the old man answered and said: "Friend, irksome were the task to recount all that the eyes may see. Many wayfarers travel by the road, on errands some of much evil, others of great good. It were hard to know each of them. But for myself, all day was I digging about the knoll of my vineyard plot. Meseemed, good sir, that I saw a boy—though I know not of a certainty —and this boy, whoe'er he was, a mere babe, was following strong-horned kine; and he carried a staff and walked from side to side. The kine he was driving backwards with their heads towards him."

So spoke the old man, but the god hearing his tale hied more quickly on his way. Now he espied a broad-winged eagle, and straightway knew that the reiver was the son of Zeus Cronion. Swiftly then did King Apollo, Son of Zeus, haste on to goodly Pylus in quest of his ambling kine, covering his broad shoulders with a purple cloud. And the Far Darter caught sight of their tracks, and spake these words: "Ye gods! surely this is a mighty wonder that mine eyes behold. Those are the tracks of my horned kine, but they are turned back to the asphodel meadow. But these are the footprints of neither man nor woman, nor of grey wolves nor bears nor lions; and it is no shaggy centaur, I trow, which with fleet hoofs maketh such monstrous tracks. Strange footprints on this side the way, stranger still on that!"

With these words King Apollo, the Son of Zeus, hasted forward. And he gat him to the wood-clad mountain Cyllené, to the deep-shadowed hollow in the rock where the ambrosial nymph gave birth to the Son of Zeus Cronion. Over the goodly hill a sweet scent was spreading, and many long-shanked sheep were at pasture on the grass. There he now hurried down the rocky ground into the dim cave —Apollo himself, the Far Darter. But when the Son of Zeus and Maia saw that Apollo, the Far Darter, was wroth about his kine, he sank within his fragrant swaddling-clothes. Like as the piled wood embers are covered by the thick ashes, so did Hermes hide himself at sight of the Far Darter. In small space he drew together head, and hands, and feet, like a new-born babe, and with his shell under his arm courted sweet sleep though full awake. But the Son of Zeus and Leto failed not to recognise the fair mountain nymph, and the little boy, her son, wrapped though he was in sly craftihood. When he had scanned each recess of the great cavern, he took a great key and opened three closets full of nectar and goodly ambrosia. Within them were lying much gold and silver, and many purple and shining garments of the nymphs, such as the hallowed homes of the Blessed Gods contain. When the Son of Leto had thus searched all the recesses of the great cave, he spake these words to glorious Hermes: "Ho! boy! thou lying there in thy cradle! tell me of my kine full quickly, or soon we twain shall quarrel beyond all seemliness. Yea, I shall take and hurl thee into murky Tartarus, into dread impenetrable darkness. Nor shall thy mother, nor yet thy father bring thee back to light, but 'neath the earth shalt thou wander a leader among men undone."

To him made answer Hermes with crafty words: "Son of Leto! what harsh word is this thou hast spoken? Is it cattle of the fields thou art come here to seek? I have neither seen nor heard of them, nor listened to another's story. I cannot tell of them, nor win the tiding-fee. In no wise am I like unto some stalwart reiver. That is no task of mine; till now I think of other things— of sleep, my mother's milk, my swaddling-clothes about my shoulders, and my warm baths. May none learn how this strife hath arisen! In sooth it would be marvel great among immortals that a child new born should cross the threshold after stall-fed oxen. Absurd is this thing thou speakest! But yesterday was I born, my feet are tender and the way is rough beneath. An thou wilt, I shall swear a great oath by my father's head. I pledge me that I neither am myself to blame, nor have I seen any other who stole your kine—whatever kine may be, of that I know but hearsay."

Thus he spake, and with many a darting glance from his eyes, he winked and looked this way and that, whistling loudly as he maintained this false tale. But with a soft laugh Far Darting Apollo addressed him: "Thou innocent! thou cunning deceiver! ofttimes, methinks, thou wilt break into goodly houses by night, and many a man wilt thou beggar by ransacking his house without noise —so knavish are thy words. And many herdsmen of the fields wilt thou harass in the mountain glens, whenas thou longest for flesh, and happenest upon the herds and the woolly sheep. Up, lest thou sleepest the last long sleep, come down from thy cradle, thou friend of dark night. This belike will be thine honour among immortals in days to come, to be yclept for ever the Robber-Lord."

Thus spake Phoebus Apollo, and took the boy in his arms. Then the doughty slayer of Argos, as he was lifted in Apollo's hands, bethought him, and let forth an "omen," a wretched belly-thrall, an insolent messenger, and straightway thereafter sneezed. Apollo heard him, and threw famous Hermes from his hands to the ground. Fain as he was for the road, he sat down afront him, and bantering Hermes addressed him thus: "Good Luck, Swaddling-bands, Son of Zeus and Maia! By these omens I shall by-and-bye find my stout beasts; and thou wilt lead the way." Thus he spake, but Cyllenian Hermes briskly rose and hasted forward. With his hands he drew up to his ears on either side the wrapping that was folded round his shoulders, and thus replied: "Whither dost thou bear me, Far Darter, most furious of all the gods? Is it for thy kine that thou dost vex me thus in thine anger? Perish the breed of cattle! Why, I neither stole your kine myself, nor have I seen the thief; whatever kine may be, of that I know but hearsay. Let our cause be tried before Zeus Cronion."

Thus were Hermes the Wanderer and the famous Son of Leto with angry hearts wrangling over all the matter at great length. Apollo, on the one hand, informed by sure augury about the kine, was holding glorious Hermes captive, but the Cyllenian god by his craft and wily words was fain to deceive the God of the Silver Bow. Albeit when Hermes found him a match for all his wiles, swiftly did he step over the sand ahead, with the

Son of Zeus and Leto behind him. Soon were they come to the heights of fragrant Olympus, these goodly sons of Zeus to their father Cronion. For there were set for the twain the scales of justice. Fair was the day on snowy Olympus, and in the wake of golden-throned dawn were the gods gathering together. In front of the knees of Zeus, Hermes and Apollo of the Silver Bow took their place. And Zeus, who thunders on high, questioned his shining son, addressing him thus : "Whence, O Phoebus, art thou driving this mighty booty, this new-born child of herald's mien ? Pressing matter this to come before the assembly of the gods." To him in reply spake the King, Far Darting Apollo: "Sire, not paltry is the tale thou soon wilt hear, though thou tauntest me as being the one lover of spoil. This boy here I found a thorough thief on Cyllené's heights, after I had fared a long way : a knave beyond all gods that I have seen, or all the robber-folks upon the earth. He stole my kine from the meadow, and drove them off at evening to the shore of the boisterous sea, making straight for Pylos. Their hoof-tracks were huge to wonderment, yea, miracles of a glorious god. For the black dust showed the steps of my kine facing towards the asphodel meadow, but this boy himself, peerless contriver, fared neither with feet nor hands over the sandy ground. Nay, by other device did he make the journey, a device as strange as if one were sandalled with toppings of the oak. So long as he followed the sandy road, right easily were all the tracks seen in the dust, but when he had crossed the great stretch of sand, the trail of the cattle and their driver became indistinct on the hard ground. Albeit a man observed him driving the herd of broad-faced kine straight towards Pylus. Now when he had stalled the kine in peace, and juggled from one side the road to the other, he laid him down in his cradle, as if wrapped in dark night, in the gloom of a murky cave. Even an eagle's keen glance would not have spied him. Ofttimes did he rub his eyes with his hands while plying his craftiness, and bluntly did he at once speak out his plea. "I have neither seen nor learned (of your kine), nor listened to another's story. I cannot tell thee of them, nor win the tiding-fee." When he had spoken thus, Phoebus Apollo sat him down, and Hermes straightway told his tale among the immortals, addressing it to Cronion, Lord of all the Gods. "Father Zeus! verily I shall tell thee sooth, for I am true and know not how to lie. To-day at sunrise came Apollo to our abode, seeking for his ambling kine. And none of the Blessed Gods did he bring to witness or to see. But he bade me speak out under great stress, and threatened much to throw me into wide Tartarus, because he forsooth weareth the tender bloom of gallant youth, whereas I am but a child of yesterday, as he himself wotteth, in no wise like unto a sturdy reiver. Believe me—for thou claimest to be my sire—I neither drove home the cattle, I pledge my happiness thereto, nor did I go over the threshold. This is sooth I tell. And I highly reverence Helios and the other gods. Yea, I love thee and fear him. Thyself dost know that I am innocent, and I shall swear a great oath thereto. By these rich portals of the gods I am not guilty; and I shall one day yet avenge me upon him for the cruel charge, strong though he be, and do thou aid the younger."

Thus spake Cyllenian Argeiphontes with a wink. And he kept his wrapping-plaid on his arm, nor cast it off. Zeus broke into loud laughter at the sight of the mischievous boy, as he gave his shrewd and clever denial about the kine. The twain he bade go seek them with one heart, Hermes as guide to lead the way, and show the place without guile where he had hidden the strong heads of kine. Cronides nodded, and glorious Hermes did his bidding, for easily doth the mind of Aegis-bearing Zeus prevail. So the twain, the goodly Son of Zeus fared in haste to sandy Pylos at the ford of the Alpheius. And they came to the pastures and the high-roofed byre, where Hermes was tending his booty in the night-tide. There Hermes forthwith gat him to the rocky cave, and drove the sturdy cattle into the light. But the Son of Leto, glancing aside, saw the hides on the high rock, and quickly made question of famous Hermes: " Thou Rogue, how hadst thou power, new-born infant as thou art, to flay two kine? Of a sooth I dread thy might hereafter; no need for thee to wax strong, Cyllenian Son of Maia!"

*Thus he spake, and with his hands Hermes began twisting strong bands of withes. And the withes were soon closely plaited together at his feet on the ground where he stood, and were placed upon all the stall-fed kine by the counsel of Thievish Hermes. Apollo was astonied at the sight. Now the strong Slayer-of-Argos with many a sidelong glance looked down at the ground, fain to cover over (his fault); and deftly did he soften to his liking the Far Darting Son of Leto, violent though he were. In his left hand he took his lyre and tuned it with his plectrum, string by string, and clearly did it sound to his hand. Thereat Phoebus Apollo laughed with joy, and the goodly tone of the divine music passed through his soul, and sweet desire laid hold of his heart as he listened. Harping sweetly on his lyre, Maia's son took courage and stood on the left of Phoebus Apollo. Anon

---

* V. 409-413. I take this difficult passage as a practical answer by Hermes to Apollo's question in 405. By reading ἄγνων in 410, we get an antecedent for τάι; and κεῖντο for ῥεῖα at the beginning of 412, a fairly satisfactory sense.

playing a clear prelude he began to sing,* and melodious was his utterance. He told of the deathless gods and the sombre earth, how at first they were, and how each god received his allotted portion. First of the gods he honoured in song Mnemosyné, mother of the Muses. For she had been allotted Maia's son. The other deathless gods, each according to dignity and birth, the noble Son of Maia honoured, telling all the ordered tale, as he struck the lyre upon his arm. But a masterful desire seized Apollo's heart within his breast, and uttering winged words he spoke to Hermes: "O Slayer of Kine, Schemer, who hast fashioned a comrade for the Feast,† herein hast thou devised the worth of fifty kine. Now meseemeth, we shall quietly make our peace. Come, pray tell me this, Ingenious Son of Maia, have these wondrous powers been thine since birth, or hath some god or mortal man gifted them—a splendid boon, and inspired thee with song divine? Wonderful is this new song I have heard! Never before, I trow, hath any known it either of men or of gods who haunt the Olympian Dwellings, save thyself, O Reiver, thou Son of Zeus and Maia. What skill! what charm against carking cares! what

---

* V. 426. ἀμβολάδην. Baumeister however, on the authority of the Scholiast to Pindar, Nem. x. 62, holds the correct interpretation to be "intentâ voce." Following him the translation would be, "Anon as he played clearly he lifted up his voice and sang."

† V. 436. Read "πονεύμενε δαιτὸς ἑταίρην."

deftness! Yea, surely all these are by, to win joy and love and sweet slumber. Comrade though I be of the Olympian Muses, the patrons of the dance, of rich minstrelsy, of swelling music and the passionate pipe-strain, yet never heretofore hath my heart taken such delight in the festive rites which attend the carles' merry-makings. Such is my wonder at thy sweet harping. Howbeit since, young as thou art, thou hast skill in glorious crafts, sit thee down, my boy, and praise the saying of thine elders. Know that soon there will be fame among the immortals for thyself and thy mother. This is sooth I shall tell. Yea, by this cornel dart I shall lead thee among the immortals honoured and glorious, and give thee splendid gifts, and fail thee not in making it good." To him Hermes made reply with cunning words: "Shrewd is thy request of me, Far Darter, and nought do I begrudge thee to master mine art. This day shalt thou know it, for fain I am to be kind to thee in rede and word, and thy mind hath good skill in all things. For first among the immortals, O Son of Zeus, thou sittest, brave and strong. And Zeus the Counsellor loveth thee with all reverence, and hath given thee glorious gifts and honours. Thou art taught in oracles they say, O Far Darter, by the voice of Zeus, for all prophecy is his. And now I myself have learned thy full prophetic power. Thy gift it is to know whatever thou desirest.

Since, then, thy heart prompteth thee to play the lyre, do thou sing, and harp and make joyaunce by gift of mine (and win me glory, friend), and take in thy hands my melodious cleared-toned comrade, which wotteth how to tell glorious things in order fair.

"Bear it hereafter boldly to rich feast, to amorous dance, and to splendid revel—a joy by night and day.

"If any trained musician doth with art and skill enquire of it, to him it giveth voice and teacheth all manner of things pleasant to the mind; but if any novice doth at first impetuously enquire of it, in vain discords will he strike the notes. Howbeit 'tis thy gift to know what thou desirest. To thee, then, shall I give this lyre, O noble Son of Zeus. And now we shall graze down the pastures of hill and fertile dale with the cattle. So shall the kine coupling with the bulls bring forth good store of calves, male and female. There is no need at all that thou, though eager for gain, shouldst be over-violent in thine anger."

With these words he held out the lyre. Phoebus Apollo took it, and placed his whip in the hands of Hermes, and entrusted to his care the herds. And the Son of Maia received them with a smile. Then the noble Son of Leto, the King, Far Darting Apollo, took the lyre on his left hand,

and with the plectrum touched it string by string. Sweetly did it sound to his hand. And the God sang in accompaniment a beautiful song.

Thereafter they turned the kine towards the lush meadow, and themselves twain, the goodly children of Zeus, hasted back again to snowy Olympus, delighting themselves with the lyre. And Zeus the Counsellor was glad. (The twain did he unite in friendship. And from that day forth Hermes loved the Son of Leto, whenas he gave as a pledge to the Far Darter the lyre he loved, and Apollo with skill played it on his arm. Himself withal did invent an art of other cunning, contriving the far heard music of the reed-pipes.) Then did the Son of Leto make speech to Hermes thus: "I fear thee, Son of Maia, Leader, Contriver, lest thou rob me of both my lyre and my bent bow. For thou hast from Zeus the honour that thou wilt establish commerce among men over the fruitful earth. Would that thou wert willing to swear the great oath of the gods (either with nod of the head, or by the many waters of Styx), that in all things thou wilt do what is kind and friendly to my heart. Then did Maia's son bend his head and pledge him never to steal what the Far Darter had, nor draw nigh his strong dwelling. And Apollo withal the Son of Leto plighted him in troth and love that none other among immortals should be dearer—nor god nor man, offspring of Zeus. "Yea, I shall make thee a perfect mediator between gods and men—trusted and precious to my own heart. And of wealth and riches I shall give thee withal a beautiful three-leaved rod of gold, which will guard thee from harm, bringing to fulfilment all the course of excellent words and deeds which I claim to have learned from the voice of Zeus. But prophecy, good Son of Zeus, for which thou askest, it is granted neither for thee nor any other immortal to learn. That is the secret of Zeus. Yea, mine own self did plight my troth and swear a mighty oath that none other of the eternal gods save myself should know the prudent counsel of Zeus. Do thou, my brother of the Golden Wand, bid me not tell the sacred purposes which far-seeing Zeus is planning. One mortal I shall ban, another bless, perplexing much the kindreds of luckless men. That man shall have profit of mine oracle, who is led to me by the cry and flight of perfect birds—yea, he shall have profit of mine oracle, and I shall not deceive him. But whoso trusteth in false birds and desireth against my will to consult mine oracle, and to know more than the ever-living gods, that man, I say, shall come a fruitless errand. Albeit I shall receive his gifts. Yet one thing shall I tell thee, Son of glorious Maia,

and Aegis-bearing Zeus, Thou god of Luck :—
There are certain Thriae, maiden sisters three,
that wanton on swift wing. Sprinkled with white
meal are their heads, and they dwell beneath the
folds of Parnassus, teachers of prophecy apart.
This art I studied even as a boy when tending
cattle, and my father heeded not. Thence they
fly hither and thither, feeding on honey-comb and
bringing all things to fulfilment. When they are
inspired with eating the yellow honey, full fain
are they to speak the truth. But if they be
robbed of the sweet food of the gods, then falsely
do they speak in mutual confusion.* These then
do I grant thee. Do thou enquire of them truly
and delight thine own heart ; and if thou shouldest
instruct any man therein, he will ofttimes listen
to thine oracle, if fortune favour him. This be
thy gift, O Son of Maia, and do thou attend
withal to the ambling cattle of the fields, and the
horses and the toiling mules. (Yea, over glaring
lions, and boars of gleaming tusks, and dogs and
sheep which the broad earth feeds), and over all
flocks be glorious Hermes lord. Let him be the
one appointed messenger to Hades, who, though
he hath received no gift,† will grant him highest
honour." Thus did King Apollo pledge the Son

---

* V. 563. Or reading, δίνο υσαι, "As they whirl about each other."
† V. 573. ἄδοτός περ ἐὼν may also be rendered "though niggard of gifts."

of Maia with all affection. And Cronion gave added favour. With all mortals and immortals doth Hermes consort. Little doth he bless, but ever through the mirk night he deceiveth the kindreds of mortal folk.

Hail to thee, O Son of Zeus and Maia, I shall remember thee and another lay.

IV.

TO APHRODITÉ.

Sing to me, O Muse, of the deeds of Golden Aphrodité, who stirreth sweet desire among the gods, and subdueth the kindreds of men who die, soaring birds, all beasts, and all the teeming broods of land and sea. Dear to them all are the deeds of fair-crowned Cytherea. But three hearts can she neither win nor beguile. Grey-eyed Athené, daughter of Aegis-bearing Zeus — *she* hath no pleasure in the deeds of golden Aphrodité. Nay, her joyaunce is in war, and the work of Ares, in onsets and combats, and the doing of doughty deeds. First was she to teach the wrights of earth to fashion wains and beautiful chariots of brass. And she teacheth glorious arts to tender maidens in the halls, inspiring the heart of each.

Nor ever doth smiling Aphrodité conquer in love clear-toned Artemis of the Golden Distaff.

For her delight is the bow, and the slaying of beasts on the mountains, the lyre, the dance, the loud halloo, the shady glen, and the city of just men.

Nor withal do the deeds of Aphrodité give pleasure to Hestia, the chaste maiden, eldest child of Cronos the Crafty (youngest too, by the counsel of Zeus the Aegis Bearer), queenly damsel whom Poseidon and Apollo wooed. Howbeit she would none of them, but stoutly refused them. Nay, she swore a great oath which verily hath been accomplished, her hand on the head of Aegis-bearing Zeus, her father—to be a virgin all her days, this goddess divine. And in the stead of wedlock Father Zeus granted her a glorious gift, and she sat her down in the heart of the hall, choosing the best portion. In all temples of the gods is she held in honour, and among all mortals is she chiefest of the gods.

Of these (three) hath Aphrodité no power to win or beguile the hearts. But of all besides there is nought that hath escaped her either of blessed gods or of men who die. Yea, she hath even led astray the mind of Zeus the Thunderer, who is the greatest, and is allotted highest honour. At her will seducing his stout heart she hath embroiled him with mortal women, eluding Hera, his sister-spouse, fairest far of immortal goddesses in beauty. Glorious daughter is she of Cronos the Crafty, and

Rheia, her mother. And Zeus the eternal Counsellor made her his chaste and dutiful wife. But into the soul of Aphrodité herself Zeus sent a sweet passion, to love a mortal man, that she too might not long be kept from mortal couch, and might not some day boast among all the gods and say with laughter sweet that she, smiling Aphrodité, had emmeshed the gods in the love of women, who had borne mortal sons to the immortals, and that she had emmeshed the goddesses with mortal men.

In her soul therefore he implanted a sweet passion for Anchises, who was then herding his cattle on the lofty heights of many-streamed Ida— handsome as the immortals. Him did smiling Aphrodité see and love, and passion took firm hold of her heart. To Cyprus she gat her and entered the fragrant temple at Paphos, where was her shrine and an odorous altar. When she was got within she put to the shining doors. There did the Graces bathe her and anoint her with ambrosial oil, such as gloweth upon the everliving gods—priceless ambrosial oil which had been offered to her. Then smiling Aphrodité, busking her body bravely in all her beautiful attire, and adorning herself with gold, hasted to Troy, leaving spicy Cyprus, high among the clouds, swiftly speeding her way. To many-streamed Ida she came—Ida, the mother of beasts. Over the mountain she fared straight for the steading.

In her train went fawning the hoary wolves and cruel lions, bears and swift leopards greedy for the hinds. At the sight her heart was glad within her, and she sent desire into their breasts. And they all laid them down in pairs in the bosky dens, but herself fared on to the well-builded huts. At the steading she found the hero Anchises left alone apart from the others, with beauty from the gods. The herdsmen were all following their oxen down the grassy pastures, but he had been left alone at the steading apart from the rest, and was wandering up and down playing clearly on the lyre. In front of him she halted—Aphrodité, Daughter of Zeus—like unto an unwedded maiden in stature and beauty, that he might not fear her when he beheld her with his eyes. Anchises at sight of her was amazed and wondered at her beauty, and stature, and shining attire. For she was clad in a robe brighter than fiery flame, and wore twisted bracelets and shining earrings. Round her smooth neck were beautiful necklaces, goodly with gold and braveries. Like the moon did her soft breast flash, a wonder to see. Love took hold of Anchises, and thus he spake to her: "Welcome, lady, whoever of the blessed ones thou art that comest to this homestead—Artemis, or Leto, or golden Aphrodité, or noble Themis, or bright-eyed Athené. Or peradventure thou art one of the Graces come hither, who attend all the gods and are hailed immortal, or one of the Nymphs who haunt the beauteous glades (or dwell on this fair mountain), the river fountains and grassy leas. To thee shall I build an altar on some height—a spot seen all round, and offer thee goodly victims all the seasons through. And be thou gracious and grant me to be excellent among the Trojans! make my stock fruitful in days to come; and to myself withal vouchsafe that in long and happy life I may gaze on the sunlight prosperous among the kindreds, and reach the threshold of old age."

To him then replied Aphrodité, daughter of Zeus: "O Anchises, noblest of earth-born men; no goddess am I, why liken me to the immortal ones? but a mortal, born of a woman. My father is Otreus, of famous name, belike thou hast heard of him, who reigneth over all fortified Phrygia. But thy speech and mine own I know well. For Trojan was the nurse who reared me in our hall, training me up from my girlhood, having received me at my mother's hands. So that with thy speech too I am well acquainted.

"Lately did Argeiphontes of the Golden Staff snatch me away from the band of clear-toned Artemis of the Golden Distaff. A many of us were sporting, nymphs and courted maidens, encircled by a countless throng; albeit from their midst Argeiphontes of the Golden Staff snatched me away. He led me over much tillage of mortal folk and over much ground untilled and unpeopled, through which among the shaded coverts range beasts of prey, and I did not even seem to touch the teeming earth.

"He foretold that by the bed of Anchises I should be a wedded wife, and bear thee noble children. And when he had shown this and spoken, verily the strong Slayer of Argos departed again among the kindreds of the immortals. But to thee have I come—mighty necessity was upon me. I beseech thee by Zeus and your good parents—no sorry folks might beget a man like thee — lead me a maiden, stranger to love, and show me to thy father and thy dutiful mother, and thy brothers born of the same stock, if belike I shall be to them an unfit daughter-in-law or not. And send a messenger speedily to the Phrygians of the Swift Steeds, to tell my father and my mother in her anxiety.

"They will send thee good store of gold, and woven raiment. Do thou take for thyself a full and splendid dower. When thou hast done this, make ready a rich wedding-feast—honourable among men and immortal gods."

With these words the goddess inspired his heart with sweet desire. Love took hold of Anchises, and thus he spake and said: "If mortal thou art and a woman bare thee, and thy sire is Otreus of famous name, as thou sayest, and thou hast come hither by the will of Hermes, the immortal Leader, and wilt be my wife for ever, then no one of gods or mortal men will here restrain me from mingling with thee now in love; not even were Far Darting Apollo himself to hurl whistling shafts from his silver bow. Yea, I should be willing, O Lady, peer of goddesses, to enter the house of Hades once I had ascended thy bed. Thus speaking he took her hand. Sweet-smiling Aphrodité turned her, and casting down her beauteous eyes crept to the well-spread couch which already had been strewn with soft rugs for the prince. Above it lay skins of bears and deep-voiced lions, which himself had slain among the tall mountains. When they had got them upon the goodly bed, he stripped from her body first its bright adornments—brooches and twisted armlets, ear-rings and chains. Next Anchises loosed her belt, and did off her shining robes, and laid them upon a silver-studded chair. Then by the will and decree of the gods he lay by the goddess, a mortal by an immortal, though he knew it not.

Now whenas the herdsmen are wearing homeward to the steading from the flowery pastures the oxen and fat sheep, she poured over Anchises a deep sound slumber, and herself did on her beautiful garments. And having done them all bravely around her body, the queenly goddess stood by the couch, and her head reached the well-builded ceiling. Immortal beauty shone from her cheeks

—the very beauty of fair-crowned Cytherea. From his slumber she awoke him, and spake to him, saying: "Arise, Son of Dardanus. Why dost thou indulge in deep slumber now? Tell me, if I seem to thee to be such as at first thou didst behold me with thine eyes."

Thus she spake. And Anchises right speedily heard her from his slumber. But when he saw the neck and fair eyes of Aphrodité, he was afraid and turned his glance aside another way. His handsome face he covered again with his cloak, and appealing to her spake winged words. "Whenas first I saw thee with mine eyes, O goddess, I wist that thou wert divine; but thou didst speak untruly. I pray thee by Zeus, the Aegis-Bearer, let me not dwell among men a living ghost! Have pity! since no man is hale who coucheth with immortal goddesses." To him then made reply Aphrodité, daughter of Zeus: "O Anchises, most glorious of mortal men! take courage, and be not overanxious in thy heart. There is no fear that thou shouldest suffer scathe from me or the other Blessed Ones, for thou art dear to the gods. Thou shalt have a dear son, who will reign among the Trojans, and children's children will ever be born to him. Aeneas will be his name, because woeful sorrow laid hold of me, when I lighted on the bed of a mortal man. The most godlike of mortal men in comeliness and stature have ever sprung from thy stock. It was for his beauty in sooth that Zeus the Counsellor ravished yellow-haired Ganymede, that he might consort with immortals, and, a marvel to behold, be cup-bearer to the gods in the house of Zeus, honoured among all the immortals, pouring ruddy nectar from a golden·beaker. But grief insatiable seized the heart of Tros, and he wist not whither the divine blast had snatched away his dear son. So he mourned for him ever unceasingly. And Zeus had compassion upon him, and as fee for his son gave him high-stepping horses, such as carry the immortals. These he gave him as a gift to keep. And at the bidding of Zeus, Argeiphontes the Messenger told him all things how his son was deathless and unageing like unto the gods. Howbeit when he heard the message of Zeus, he grieved no more, and his heart was glad within, and joyfully drave he the wind-swift steeds.

So too Golden-Throned Eōs carried away Tithonus of your race, a peer of the immortals. She betook her to Cronion of the Dark Clouds, to pray that he should be deathless and live for ever. And Zeus consented, and granted her desire.

Short-sighted was queenly Eōs, nor wotted she in her heart to ask for youth, and to get rid of accursed eld.

Whileas winsome youth was his, in joyaunce of Eōs, the Golden-Throned, Daughter of Mist, he abode by the streams of Oceanus at the world's edge. And when the first gray hairs streamed from his fair head and noble chin, of sooth the queenly Eōs withdrew from his bed, though she kept and cherished him in her halls with food and ambrosia, and gave him beautiful garments. But when loathsome eld weighed sorely upon him, and he could in no wise move or raise his limbs, this counsel seemed in her heart to be best. She laid him down in a chamber, and put to the shining doors. And his voice floweth on unceasingly, but there is no strength, as of yore there was, in his supple limbs. "I would not have thee in such frailty to be deathless, and to live for ever among the immortals. If thou couldest live with all thy beauty and stature, and be my husband, grief would not then lap round my shrewd heart. But as it is ruthless eld—the common lot—will speedily lap thee round; eld which one day bideth by men, woeful, and weary, and hated of the gods. And I shall have great dishonour on thine account, for ever and aye among the immortal gods, who aforetime trembled at the words and wiles by which I erstwhile embroiled all immortal gods with mortal women, for my purpose mastered all. But now no longer will my mouth ope to tell this forth among immortals, for deep hath been my folly, sore and nameless, and I have wandered from my wits, and couching with a man I have conceived a son.

That son, when first he beholdeth the sunlight, the deep-bosomed mountain Nymphs will nurture, they who haunt this great and fertile mountain, and are numbered neither among mortals nor immortals. With them the Sileni and the keen-eyed Argeiphontes mingle in love, in the shelter of charming caves. At their birth there sprang up also on the fruitful earth, pines or tall-crested oaks, fair and luxuriant. On the tall hill-sides they stand facing the sun. Groves of the gods they are called. Never do mortals fell them with the axe. But whenso death's doom is nigh, the fair trees first wither on the ground, their bark around them dies, and the twigs drop off. And at the same time the soul of the Nymphs leaveth the light of the Sun. These Nymphs will keep my son and rear him in their midst. But that I may tell thee all that is in my mind, in the fifth year I shall come to thee again with thy son. So soon as thou beholdest with thine eyes thy child, thou wilt be glad at the sight; for godlike indeed will he be. Straightway thou wilt lead him to windy Ilium. And if any man shall ask thee what mother bore thy dear son, remember to answer him as I bid thee. Say that he is thy child by one of the blushing Nymphs who haunt this wood-clad hill. But if thou tell and boast with foolish mind, that thou hast met in love the fair crowned Cytherea, Zeus in his wrath will strike thee with a lurid bolt. All is told thee.

Be prudent of heart. Restrain thyself, and speak not my name, but fear the anger of Heaven."

Thus having spoken, she sprang up to the breezy sky.

Farewell, O Goddess, Queen of fair-builded Cyprus. Having honoured thee first, I shall pass to another hymn.

V.

TO DEMETER.

Of fair haired Demeter, goddess revered, I begin my song—of the goddess and her long-ancled daughter, whom the King of Hades stole away with the sanction of Zeus, the far-seeing Thunderer, from Demeter of the Golden Sword, the Fruitful. She was sporting with the deep-bosomed daughters of Ocean, and gathering flowers over the lush mead—the rose, the crocus, the beautiful violet, the iris, and the hyacinth—the narcissus too, which Earth by the counsel of Zeus brought forth to favour Polydectes, a lure to the dimpled maid. Wondrous was its bloom, a marvel to the sight of all, both deathless gods and mortal men. From its roots withal there shot out a hundred heads, and at its fragrant scent laughed all the wide welkin above, and all the land, and the salt sea wave. The maiden in wonder stretched out her hands, the twain together, to take the beauteous treasure; when the broad-wayed Earth yawned along the Mysian Plain, and up sprang King Polydegmon, the worshipful Son of Kronos, with his immortal steeds. He seized her all unwilling, and on his golden car bore her away lamenting. Loud she shrieked with her voice, calling on Father Cronides, the highest and best. But no immortal and no mortal heard her voice, nor did the fruitful Mead-Nymphs. Only the tender-hearted daughter of Persaeus, dainty-snooded Hecate, heard from her cave, and Helios the king, noble Son of Hyperion, when the maiden called on Father Cronides. But away from the gods was he seated, apart in his temple, where suppliants throng, receiving beautiful gifts from mortal men.

Unwilling was Persephone, but her father's brother, Sovran and Lord of all, many-named Son of Kronos, with the abetting of Zeus, bore her away on his immortal steeds. While the goddess beheld the Earth, the starry sky, the restless teeming sea, and the beams of the Sun, and still hoped to see her dear mother, and the tribes of eternal gods, so long did hope cheer her great heart, grief-stricken though she were.

The mountain peaks and the depths of the sea echoed with her divine voice, and her queenly mother heard it. A sharp pang seized her heart, and she rent with her dear hands the wimple round her ambrosial locks, and cast from her shoulders twain the sea-blue veil, then like a bird hasted in search of her, over dry land and sea. None of the gods or of mortal men could tell her truly, and no omen came to her with soothfast tidings. Nine days did queenly Dēo wander over the earth, blazing torch in hand, nor ever in her grief did she taste ambrosia and sweet nectar, or lay her body in the bath. But when the tenth light-spreading morn had come, Hecaté met her, torch in hand, and with tidings to tell, spake and addressed her.

"Queenly Demeter, Bringer of Seasons, Rich in Gifts, what heavenly god or mortal man hath snatched away Persephone and vexed thy dear heart? Her voice I heard, but mine eyes beheld not who he was. Speedily let me tell thee all the truth." . . .

Thus spake Hecaté. With no words did the Daughter of fair-tressed Rheia make reply, but swiftly along with her darted forth blazing torch in hand. To Helios they gat them, the sentinel of gods and men, and halted afront his steeds, and the glorious goddess questioned him.

"O Helios, pity me* by thy sight, if ever by word or deed I have cheered thy heart and soul. The daughter whom I bore, a scion sweet, in beauty excellent—oft did I hear her voice through the barren sky as of one being ravished, albeit mine

* V. 64. Or reading θεᾶς ὕπερ, "For a goddess' sake."

eyes beheld her not. But thou gazest with thy beams over all the land and sea from the clear welkin, do thou tell me truly of my daughter dear —if thou hast seen her anywhere—what god or mortal man hath taken her away from me, forcing an unwilling maid."

Thus she spake. And the son of Hyperion made answer:—"Daughter of Fair-tressed Rheia, Queen Demeter, thou shalt know. Greatly do I respect and pity thee in thy grief for thy lissom daughter. None other of the gods is to blame, save Cloud-Gathering Zeus, who gave her to his brother Hades to be his cherished spouse. And Hades with his steeds hath carried her off, shrieking loudly, under the murky darkness. But, goddess, stay thy loud lament. In no wise is there need that thy wrath should be terrible. No unfit son-in-law among the gods hast thou in Hades, Lord of All, thy brother of one lineage. And for honour he won the right, when first the threefold division was made, to be lord of those among whom he dwelleth."

Thus speaking he called to his steeds, and they at his bidding swiftly bore on his speeding chariot, like broad-pinioned birds. But a pang more dire and cruel entered her heart. Wroth then at Cronion of the Dark Clouds, she forsook the assembly of the gods and lofty Olympus, and gat her to the cities and rich farms of men, long time disguising her form. Nor did any man or deep-bosomed woman ken her by sight till she came to the house of wise Celeus, who then was lord of fragrant Eleusis. By the wayside she sat her down, sore in heart, at the Maiden Well, where the townsfolks gat them water, in the shadow where over her head grew an olive thicket. In semblance she was like unto an aged woman who is bereft of child-bearing and the gifts of garland-loving Aphrodité. Such are the nurses to the children of doom-giving kings, and the housekeepers in their echoing halls. The daughters of Celeus of Eleusis saw her as they went after the easily drawn water, that they might bear it in golden pitchers to their father's house. Four godlike damsels in the flower of maidenhood, Callidicé, Cleisidicé, lovely Demo, and Callithöe who was eldest of them all. They knew her not—the gods are hard for men to recognise—but standing near they addressed to her winged words:—

"Who of aged folk and whence art thou, old dame? And why hast thou wandered from the city and art not nigh the dwellings, where there are women of thine own age, and women younger too, who would welcome thee both with word and deed?" Thus spake they, and the queenly goddess made answer in words. "Hail dear children, whoever of women ye are. To you I shall tell my story. In no wise unseemly is it to speak the truth to your questioning. Dōs is my name—my lady mother gave it. From Crete have I just come over the broad back of the sea by no wish of mine. With main force and all against my will did pirate folks bear me away. With their swift ship did they in time touch at Thoricus, where the women thronged ashore and the pirates too. And they made them ready a meal in the after parts of the vessel. But my heart had no longing after sweet food. Stealthily I set out over the dark mainland, and fled from my insolent masters, that they might not by selling me, an unbought slave, enjoy my price. Thus have I got hither in my wandering, and I wot not what land this is, or who abide herein. To you may all the dwellers in Olympian palaces grant husbands to wed, and children to bear, as parents wish. But pity me, maidens! be gracious, children dear! till I am come to the house of man or woman, that I may zealously perform for them what tasks befit an aged dame. I could both carry in mine arms a new-born babe and nurse it well, and watch the house, and spread my master's bed in a recess of the strong-builded chambers, and could teach women folk their tasks."

So spake the goddess. And straightway in reply made answer the pure maiden Callidicé, fairest in beauty of Celeus' daughters.

"Good woman, we must needs bear the gifts of

Heaven despite our grief, for Heaven is stronger far. This clear hint, however, shall I give thee, and name the men on whom resteth great weight of honour here, who lead the people, and by their counsels and right dooms protect the city's ramparts—Triptolemus the shrewd in counsel, Diocles, Polyxenus, blameless Eumolpus, Dolichus, and our noble sire. All their wives manage in their households, and not one of them would at first sight scorn thy look and drive thee from her halls. Nay, they will welcome thee, for godlike indeed thou art. But if thou wilt, abide here that we may go to our father's house, and tell all fully to our mother, deep-bosomed Metaneira, if haply she may bid thee come to our own house and not search after the dwellings of others. A dear son born in her age is being reared in her strong hall—a child of prayers and gladness. If thou couldest nurse him till he reach the fulness of youth, readily would any of womankind who saw thee be envious, so many nurse-gifts would she give thee."

Thus she spake, and the goddess nodded assent. And the maidens filled their bright vessels with water, and bore them with pride. Soon they were come to the great house of their father, and quickly did they tell their mother all they had seen and heard. And she bade them go speedily and call the dame at a generous wage. Like deer or heifers in spring-time, that gambol over the lea when they have sated their desire with food, they kilt the folds of their fair garments and dart along the furrowed waggon-road. And their tresses waved over their shoulders like crocus flowers.

They found the glorious goddess by the way-side where erst they left her, and forthwith led her to their father's house. She walked behind them with stricken heart, veiling her head, and her dark robe curved round her divine tender feet. Soon they reached the house of god-born Celeus, and passed through the portico where their lady mother sat beside the lintel of the strong-builded dwelling, with her child, a young blossom, at her breast. To her side the maidens hasted, but the goddess set her feet upon the threshold, and her head reached the roof beam, and she filled the doors with a light divine. Then wonder, awe, and wan fear seized the mother, and she gave place to the goddess on the chair and bade her be seated. But Demeter, Bringer of Seasons, Generous Giver, would not be seated on the shining chair, but remained silent, casting down her beautiful eyes, till Iambé, the shrewd in wit, placed for her a strong stool, and cast over it a silver fleece. Then sitting down she drew her wimple over her with her hands, and for a long time sat speechless on her stool, nor greeted any one with word or gesture. Smileless she sat, tasting nor food nor drink, wasting away from yearning for her deep-bosomed daughter, till Iambé, the shrewd in wit, with many a bantering jest won the hallowed lady round to smile and laugh and wear a kindly mood. She too in after times also soothed away her frenzies.

To the goddess Metaneira offered a cup, filling it with honeyed wine, but she refused it, saying that it was not right for her to drink red wine. Howbeit she bade them mix meal and water with soft mint for her drink. And Metaneira made the posset, and gave it to the goddess as she ordered. Queenly Dēo took it, and made the due libation. Therewithal fair-girdled Metaneira began these words: "Welcome, dame, for I trow that thou art not of mean but of noble parentage, since reverence and favour beseem thine eyes, as the eyes of doom-giving kings. Heaven's gifts despite our grief we mortals needs must bear, for the yoke is laid upon our necks. But now, that thou art come hither, all mine shall be thine. Nurse this my boy, whom the gods gave me in mine age beyond my hope—this child of many prayers. If thou rear him and he reach the fulness of youth, then verily any of womankind who sees thee will be envious for the many nurse gifts I should give thee." To her in reply spake fair-garlanded Demeter, "All hail to thee also, Lady! Heaven grant thee blessings! Gladly shall I receive thy child, to nurse him as thou biddest. Never, I ween, by the folly of his nurse shall either witchery harm him or noxious herb. For I know a great antidote stronger than poison, and a goodly safeguard against baneful witchery."

Thus speaking she took the child in her fragrant bosom and arms divine, and the mother's heart was glad. So the goddess nursed in the halls the noble son of warlike Celeus—Demophoon, whom fair-girdled Metaneira bore. And he waxed strong like unto a god, albeit he neither ate food nor was suckled with his mother's milk. But by day Demeter anointed him with ambrosia like the child of some deity, breathing sweetness over him, and carrying him at her bosom. By night she would hide him in the might of fire like a brand, without the ken of his dear parents. To them it was marvel great, how he thrived and grew, and was like the gods to see. And ageless and deathless would she have made him, had not fair-girdled Metaneira in her folly watched by night from her fragrant chamber, and espied her. Raising a cry she smote both her thighs in terror for her son, and sore was she troubled in heart, and wailed forth winged words. "My child, Demophoon! the strange woman concealeth thee in a great fire, and worketh grief and bitter cares for me." Thus spake she in lament, and the queenly goddess heard her. And in wrath fair-garlanded Demeter drew out from the fire her dear son whom she bore in the halls when hope was past, and with divine hands laid him from her on the ground, deep anger at her heart. And at the same time she spake to fair-girdled Metaneira. "Silly mortals! witless to forecast the weird either of coming good or ill! Verily by thy folly thou hast worked mischief irremediable. Know by the ruthless waters of Styx (the oath of the gods), that immortal and ageless for ever should I have made thy son, and won him eternal honour. But now it is impossible that he should escape death and doom. Howbeit eternal honour will ever rest upon him because he hath mounted my knees and slept in mine arms. In his manhood's prime, when years have rolled, the sons of the Eleusinians long while will be joining battle and raising the dread war cry against the Athenians. . . .

"I am honoured Demeter, sovran help and joy to gods and men. Come, let all the people build me a great temple, and an altar near it, below the citadel and its high wall, on the jutting cliff above Callichorus. And in person I shall teach my rites, that hereafter by their pious fulfilment ye may appease my heart." With these words the goddess changed her size and shape, throwing off old age and breathing beauty all around her. A fragrance sweet diffused itself from her scented robe, and far shone the divine gleam from her immortal flesh, her yellow hair lay over her shoulders, and with her brightness as with levin the strong house was filled. Through the hall she passed, and straightway the mother's knees were loosed, and long time was she speechless, and remembered not her darling child to raise him from the floor. But his sisters heard his piteous cry, and leapt from their soft couches. One took up the child in her arms and laid him in her bosom, another lit a fire, and a third hasted with tender feet to raise her mother from the scented chamber. And gathering around they lovingly bathed the panting boy, but his heart was not soothed, for poorer now were the nurses and handmaids who held him.

Through the livelong night the women, quivering with fear, prayed to the glorious goddess. And at daydawn they told truly to Celeus the Mighty all the bidding of the goddess, fair-garlanded Demeter. And he summoned to the assembly the countless people, and bade them raise a rich temple and an altar to fair-tressed Demeter on the jutting cliff. The people speedily obeyed him, and hearkened to his words, and builded as he commanded: and the child waxed strong by the will of the goddess. Now when they were finished and rested from their labour, they set out each man for his home, but yellow-haired Demeter sat her down apart from all the blessed ones, and abode there wasting away with longing for her deep-bosomed daughter, and a terrible and cruel year did she make for men over the all-nourishing earth, and no seed yielded the land, for fair-garlanded Demeter destroyed it. Many a crooked plough did the oxen drag through the furrows in vain, and fruitlessly did much white barley fall in the earth. Now had she utterly destroyed the race of speech-gifted mortals by sore famine, and robbed the Dwellers in Olympus of the glorious honour of gifts and sacrifices, had Zeus not observed and taken counsel in his heart. First did he send Iris of the Golden Wing to summon fair-haired Demeter, the winsome in beauty. This his bidding; and she obeyed Zeus Cronion, the Dark Clouded, and sped with swift foot through the space between. To the town of incense-breathing Eleusis she came and found dark-robed Demeter in the temple, and addressing her, spake winged words. "O Demeter! Father Zeus, whose purposes are eternal, biddeth thee to join the tribes of immortal gods. Come then, and let not my behest from Zeus be unaccomplished." Thus she spake beseeching, but the heart of the goddess yielded not. Again thereafter the Father sent forth to her all the ever-living and blessed gods, and they hied in turns and summoned her, and offered her many beautiful gifts, and such honours as she would choose to receive among immortals. Howbeit none was able to influence her mind and purpose, for her heart was wroth, and she stoutly refused all their offers. Yea, she maintained that never would she set foot upon fragrant Olympus, never send up the fruit from the earth till her eyes beheld the fair face of her daughter.

When far-glancing Zeus, the Deep Thunderer, heard this, he sent to Erebus Argeiphontes of the Golden Wand, that by winning over Hades with soft words he might bring hallowed Persephoné from the murky darkness to the gods in light, and so her mother might behold her with her eyes, and abate her anger. Hermes disobeyed not, but swiftly sprang down under earth's recesses, leaving the home of Olympus. He found the king within his palace seated on a couch with his chaste wife, who was repining sorely from longing for her mother. And that mother with overmastering passion was still wroth at the counsel of the blessed gods. Standing near him the stout Slayer of Argos made speech: "O Hades of the Dark Hair, Lord of the dead, Father Zeus biddeth me lead queenly Persephoné forth from Erebus among the gods, that her mother may behold her with her eyes, and cease from her anger and fell wrath against the immortals. For she is compassing a grievous deed—the ruin of the strengthless tribes of earth-born folk, by burying the seed beneath the earth, and minishing the honours of the gods. Fell is her rage, and she consorteth not with the gods, but sitteth aloof within her fragrant temple, tarrying in the steep town of Eleusis."

Thus he spake. And a smile rose on the brow of Aidoneüs the Nether Prince, nor was he disobedient to the hests of King Zeus, but speedily gave bidding to wise Persephoné:

"Go, Persephoné, to thy dark-robed mother, with gentle temper and spirit in thy breast, and lose not heart far beyond all others. Among the immortals I shall be no unfit husband for thee, full brother as I am of Father Zeus. While here thou wilt be mistress of all living and creeping things, and highest honours shalt thou have among the gods. Eternal will be the vengeance upon evil doers who court not thy might with sacrifices, offering them with all due rites, and presenting acceptable gifts." Thus he spake, and sedate Persephoné was glad, and quickly leapt up for joy. But Hades, unobserved, gave her to eat a sweet pomegranate seed, administering it that she might not all her days remain on earth beside revered Demeter of the Dark Robe. Then before her eyes Aidoneüs, Lord of All, yoked his divine steeds to the golden car. Persephoné mounted the car, and by her side the strong Slayer of Argos took the reins and whip in his hands, and urged the horses forth from the palace. Naught unwilling did the twain speed on. And swiftly did they cover the long way, nor did sea, or streams of water, or grassy dells or cliffs check the speed of the divine horses, but above them they cleft the deep air in their progress. In front of the fragrant temple he drave them and pulled them up where fair-crowned Demeter dwelt. And she at the sight darted forth like a Maenad from a shady mountain forest.

(Lines 387-395 corrupt.)

"And with myself, and thy father, Dark-Clouded Cronion, thou wilt dwell, honoured among all the immortals. But if thou hast eaten, thou wilt return and dwell 'neath earth's recesses for one third part of the year's seasons, the other two with me and the other immortals. And when the earth burgeons with its many fragrant spring flowers, then from the misty darkness thou wilt arise again, a great wonder to gods and mortal men. . . .

"And by what guile did mighty Polydegmon deceive thee?"

To her in answer spake beauteous Persephoné: "Verily, mother, I shall tell thee all the truth. When Hermes, Bringer of Luck, Swift Messenger, came to me from Father Cronides, and the other Dwellers in Heaven, to lead me from Erebus, that beholding me with thine eyes thou mightest abate thy wrath and fell anger against the immortals, straightway I leaped up for joy. But Hades, unobserved, gave me the sweet morsel of a pomegranate seed, and made me eat thereof all against my will. How he snatched me away by the shrewd counsel of Cronides, my sire, and bore me under earth's recesses, I shall tell thee, and recount all the tale as thou askest. We were all of us on the pleasant lea, Leucippé, and Phaeno, Electra, and Ianthé, and Melita, and Iaché, and Rhodeia, and Callirhoë, and Melobosis, and Lyché, and blushing Ocyrrhoe, and Chryseis, and Janeira, and Acasté, and Admeté, and Rhodopé, and Plouto, and lovely Calypso, and Styx, and Urania, and beautiful Galaxauré. There were we sporting and culling with our hands the charming flowers, bunches of fair crocus, and iris and hyacinth, and rosebuds and lilies a wondrous sight, and narcissus which the wide earth bore a fell enticement. In delight was I gathering them when the earth gave way beneath me, and forth leaped the King, mighty Polydegmon. Off he carried me under the earth in his golden chariot, though I struggled much, and loudly did I shout and cry. Herein despite my grief do I tell thee all the truth."

In this wise that livelong day did they in harmony greatly cheer each other's hearts and spirits with love. Their minds were ceasing from sorrow, and mutual joys did they receive and give. And to their side came Hecaté of the Soft Sword, and oft did she embrace Demeter's hallowed daughter. Henceforth she was her royal handmaid and attendant. But far-glancing Zeus, the Deep Thunderer, sent a messenger to them—fair-haired

Rheia, to bring dark-robed Demeter among the tribes of the gods, and pledged himself to grant her whatsoever honours she should choose among the immortals. He promised withal that her daughter should dwell for the third part of the circling year under the murky darkness, and for two-thirds with her mother and the other gods. Thus he spake, and the goddess did not disregard the behests of Zeus. Fleet she sped down from the peaks of Olympus and came to Rarium, erstwhile a teeming fruitful land, but then in no wise fruitful. Fallow and leafless all it lay, and hidden was the white barley by the schemes of fair-ancled Demeter. Howbeit it was, anon, with the waxing spring, to burgeon with tall corn-ears, and the fat ground furrows were to be heavy with grain, and the corn to be bound in sheaf bands. There did she first set foot from the unharvested air. With joy did the goddesses behold each other, and glad were they at heart. And thus did Rheia of the Dainty Snood address Demeter: "Hark thee, child, Far-glancing Zeus, the Deep Thunderer, calleth thee to come among the tribes of the gods, and pledgeth him to grant thee whatsoever honours thou wilt choose among the immortals. And he hath promised that thy daughter will abide for one-third part of the circling year under the murky darkness, but for two parts with thyself and the other gods. Thus hath he vouched that it shall be, and given his pledge with his nod. Come then, my Child, obey him, and be not too unrelenting in thy wrath against Dark-Clouded Cronion. And speedily do thou bless the fruit that giveth life to men."

Thus she spake, and fair-garlanded Demeter did not disregard her. Speedily did she send up the fruitage from the rich loam, and all the wide land was heavy with leaves and flowers. And she hasted and revealed to the doom-giving kings, Triptolemus and horse-taming Diocles, and mighty Eumolpus, and Celeus, Leader of the People, the function of her rites, and enjoined on all her august mysteries, which none may violate or search into or expound, since a great curse from the gods checks the voice. Happy that earth-born man who hath beheld them! He who is not initiate and hath no part therein, never hath equal lot even when dead beneath the mouldy darkness.

Now when the queenly goddess had imparted all her rites, they went on their way to Olympus to the assembly of the gods, their peers. There they dwell, august and venerable, in the presence of Zeus, who delighteth in thunder. Blest indeed is the earth-born man whom they graciously love. Speedily do they send as a guest to his great hall, Plutus, who giveth to mortals abundance.

Come now, ye guardians of the land of incense-breathing Eleusis, and of sea-washed Paros, and rocky Antron, Queen Deō, revered and generous Bringer of the Seasons—thyself and thy daughter, beauteous Persephoné! Of your favour grant me pleasant life in return for my minstrelsy. And I shall remember thee and another lay.

VI.

TO APHRODITÉ.

Of beautiful Aphrodité, the revered, the golden crowned, shall I sing, who is mistress of the heights of all sea-washed Cyprus, where on the light foam the might of the moist-blowing Zephyr bore her over the wave of the boisterous sea. Gladly did the Golden-snooded Hours welcome her, and clothe her round with raiment divine. Upon her immortal head they set a fair and shapely crown of gold, and in her boréd ears jewels of orichalcum and precious gold. Her soft neck and white bosom they decked about with the golden chains wherewithal the Golden-snooded Hours themselves were adorned when they went to the charming dance of the gods and the hall of their sire. Now when they had set all the braveries on her person, they led her to the immortals. And they at sight of her gave greeting, and welcomed her with their hands, and longed each one of them to have her for his spouse and lead her home, admiring the beauty of Cytherea the Violet-crowned. Hail!

winsome goddess of the glancing eyes! Grant me to gain the victory in this contest, and adorn my lay. Then I shall both remember thee and another lay.

VII.

DIONYSUS, OR THE PIRATES.

Of Dionysus, son of glorious Semelé, I shall sing, how by the shore of the harvestless sea he revealed himself on a jutting foreland like unto a youth in his heyday. Beauteous dark tresses waved around him, and on his stalwart shoulders he wore a purple mantle. Erelong some rovers in a trim galley hove in sight, speeding over the wine-dark sea—Tyrrhenian folks guided by an evil fate. At sight of him they nodded to each other and hastily leaped ashore. And quickly did they seize him, and set him aboard their ship with exulting hearts. For they said among themselves that he was the son of god-born kings, and would have bound him with cruel fetters. But the fetters held him not, and the withes fell off his hands and feet afar. And with a smile in his dark eyes he sate him down. The boatswain saw it, and straightway called to his comrades and said: "Fools! what god is this ye have seized, and are fettering in his strength? Our trim vessel cannot even hold him. Of a sooth he is either Zeus, or Apollo of the Silver

Bow, or Poseidon, for he is like not unto mortal men, but to the gods who dwell in the Olympian halls. Come! let us forthwith land him again on the dark shore. And lay no hands upon him lest in his wrath he rouse tempestuous winds and a great hurricane." Thus did he speak, but the captain chid him with stinging words: "Sirrah! see thou to the wind, take hold of all the ship's ropes together, and haul up her main sail. This fellow the crew will look after. He will come, I trow, either to Egypt or to Cyprus, or to the Hyperboreans, or further still. And one day at length he will tell us of his friends, and all his gear, and of his brethren, for heaven hath put him into our hands." Thus having spoken he got the mast and mainsail of the vessel hauled up, the wind bellied out the sail, and they made taut the ropes all round. But soon strange wonders were revealed to them. First there gushed through all the dark ship a sweet odorous wine, and an ambrosial fragrance rose. Amazement laid hold on all the sailors at the sight. And anon by the sail-tops there stretched out a vine on either side, with many a hanging cluster. Round the mast dark ivy wound itself, sprouting with blossoms, and fair fruit burst forth upon it. And all the thole-pins had garlands. At the sight the sailors at last bade the pilot bring the vessel near the shore. But on board the god changed for them into a grim lion at the bow, and roared loudly. And amidship, showing wonders, he created a grisly bear, and it stood expectant. Grim and terrible glared the lion on the high deck. The men rushed in terror to the stern, and round the honest pilot stood panic-stricken. But suddenly the lion sprang forth and seized the captain; and the crew one and all, shunning a terrible doom, leaped overboard together into the awful sea, and were changed into dolphins. But the god taking pity on the pilot, held him back, and gave him all happiness, and said: "Take heart, good pilot, dear to my soul! I am blustering Dionysus, whom my mother, Cadmean Semelé, bore to the embraces of Zeus."

Hail! Son of beauteous Semelé! The man who forgetteth thee can never compose sweet song.

VIII.
TO ARES.

Mighty Ares, Charioteer of the Golden Helmet, stout-hearted Shield Bearer, brazen-clad Guardian of cities, Strong of hand, and Unwearied, Valiant Spearman, Rampart of Olympus, Sire of triumphant Victory, Champion of Justice, Lord of thy foes, Leader of righteous men, Prince of Valour, thou that whirlest thy red sphere among the seven wandering stars of the sky, where thy fiery steeds ever carry thee above the third orbit! Hear me, O Helper of Mortals, Giver of gallant youth, and shed a calm light from on high upon my life and warlike strength, that I may be able to drive away woeful evil from my head, and to guide by wisdom the erring impulse of my soul, and check the keen force of passion, which spurs me on to engage in chilling battle. Do thou, O Blessed God, grant me strength to abide in the painless laws of peace, avoiding the battle din of enemies and violent death!

IX.
TO ARTEMIS.

Sing, O Muse of Artemis, sister and nurse-mate of Apollo the Far Darter, Virgin Huntress, who having watered her teamsters at rush-grown Meles, swiftly drives her golden car through Smyrna to vine-clad Claros, where Apollo of the Silver Bow sitteth waiting for the far-shooting Huntress.

Hail to thee, and to all the goddesses with thee, in this my song! I shall first begin my hymning with thee, and beginning with thee shall pass to another lay.

X.
TO APHRODITÉ.

I shall sing of Cytherea, daughter of Cyprus, who giveth honeyed gifts to men, and her lovely face

ever smileth and weareth the bloom of beauty.*
Hail, O Goddess, queen of goodly Salamis and
all Cyprus, grant me sweet minstrelsy, and I shall
remember thee and another lay.

XI.

TO ATHENÉ.

Of Pallas Athené, the Terrible, I begin to sing, the Saviour of Cities, who careth for the deeds of war, falling cities, the battle din and the onset, and who saveth the host as they go and return. Hail to thee, goddess! vouchsafe to me fortune and happiness.

XII.

TO HERA.

I sing of Hera of the Golden Throne, whom Rheia bore, Queen of the Immortals, excellent in beauty, sister and spouse of Zeus the Thunderer, the glorious one whom all the blessed throughout wide Olympus honour and reverence equally with Zeus, who delighteth in thunder.

---

* * H. x. 3. "καὶ ἐφ' ἱμερτὸν φέρει ἄνθος." This translation suits the context, but somewhat strains the meaning of φέρω. The other rendering would be, "And she bringeth the sweet blossom of youth (to men)."

XIII.

TO DEMETER.

I begin a song to Demeter, the Fair-tressed, Revered Goddess, to herself and her daughter, beautiful Persephoné.

Hail, O Goddess! Save this city, and lead off my song.

XIV.

TO THE MOTHER OF THE GODS.

Of the Mother of all Gods and men sing to me, O clear-voiced Muse, Daughter of Mighty Zeus. Her delight is in the rattle of castanet and drum, mingled with the piping of lutes, in the howling of wolves and glaring lions, and in the echoing hills and woodland haunts.

Hail to thee, and to all the goddesses with thee, in this my song!

XV.

TO HERACLES OF THE LION HEART.

I shall sing of Heracles, the Son of Zeus, whom Alcmené bare in beautiful Thebes from the embraces of Dark-clouded Cronion—far the bravest of earth-born men. Aforetime he wandered over the vast earth and sea at the bidding of King Eurystheus, and by his own hand wrought many a doughty deed and endured much suffering, but now in the fair resort of snowy Olympus he dwelleth in joy with lissom Hebé for his wife.

Hail, O Prince, Son of Zeus, grant to me valour and wealth.

XVI.
TO ASCLEPIUS.

Of Asclepius, Healer of diseases, I begin to sing, the Son of Apollo, whom Divine Coronis, daughter of King Phlegyas, bore in the Dotian plain—a joy to men and a charmer of woeful pains. Hail to thee, O Prince! I pray to thee in song.

XVII.
TO THE DIOSCURI.

Sing, O clear-voiced Muse, of Castor and Pollux, and Polydeuces, the sons of Tyndarus, who were begotten of Olympian Zeus. Them did queenly Leda bring forth under the peaks of Taygetus, after secret dalliance with dark-clouded Cronion. Hail, ye sons of Tyndarus, who ride upon nimble steeds!

XVIII.
TO HERMES.

I sing of Cyllenian Hermes, Slayer of Argos, Lord of Cyllene and Pastoral Arcadia, Luck-bringing Messenger of the Immortals, whom Maia, the revered daughter of Atlas, bore after the love embraces of Zeus. She shunned the gathering of the Blessed Gods, abiding in a dusky cave. There did Cronion make love to the fair-haired nymph at the dead of night, when sweet sleep was holding white-armed Hera. And immortal gods and mortal men knew nought thereof.

Hail to thee, Son of Zeus and Maia! Having begun with thee, I shall pass to another hymn.

XIX.

TO PAN.

Tell me, O Muse, of the dear Son of Hermes, the Goat-footed, the Twin-horned, the Musical. He haunteth the wooded leas with the dancing nymphs that tread the crowns of steep rock calling upon Pan, the pastoral god, long haired and squalid, who is lord of every snowy ridge, of the mountain peaks and the rocky paths. Hither and thither he fareth through the thick underwoods, now sitting by quiet streams, now wandering among the steep crags, climbing the loftiest height that overlooks the flocks. Oft he courseth over the long white hills, and oft with keen glance he chargeth over the uplands, slaying the wild beast. And anon he pipeth all alone as he returns from the chase, playing blithe sweet strains on the reeds. In melody not even that bird would surpass him, which among the leaves of blossoming spring pours forth its lament in gush of honeyed song.

And again the clear-voiced mountain nymphs with nimble feet escort him, and sing by the dark water springs. And the echo sighs over the mountain top. The god glides now to right, now to left, in the dance, and now to the centre, and foots it in many a step.* On his shoulders he weareth a tawny lynx's skin, and he delighteth his heart with the strains of music in the lush meadow, where crocus and fragrant hyacinth bloom in blended confusion with the grass.

The nymphs chaunt of the blessed gods and lofty Olympus. And above all do they sing of Hermes, the Luck-bringer, how he is the swift messenger of all the gods, and how he came to many-streamed Arcadia, mother of flocks, where he hath a shrine as Lord of Cyllené. Here, god as he was, he shepherded rough-fleeced flocks in the service of a mortal man. For a longing desire had stolen upon him to enjoy the love of the fair-haired daughter of Dryops. He brought to accomplishment love's nuptials, and the nymph bore to Hermes in the halls a dear son, from the first a marvel to the eyes,

* V. 23. Or "arranges many a step."

goat-footed, twin-horned, musical, and sweetly laughing. And the mother springing up, fled and left her child; for when she saw his uncouth bearded face she was afraid. But straightway, Luck-bringing Hermes received him to his arms, and the god rejoiced exceedingly in heart. Speedily he hied to the homes of the immortals, covering the boy with the thick skins of the mountain hare. Beside Zeus and the other immortals he sat him down, and shewed his son. And all the gods were delighted in heart—none more than Bacchan Dionysus. They called him Pan, because he had made merry *all* their minds.

Hail, O Prince! To thee I pray in song. And I shall remember thee and another lay.

XX.

TO HEPHAESTUS.

Sing, O tuneful Muse! of deft Hephaestus. He with bright-eyed Athené taught glorious crafts to men on earth, who aforetime dwelt like beasts in mountain caves. But now trained in arts by the famous wright Hephaestus, they spend their lives in their homes with ease and comfort, the whole year through. Be gracious, O Hephaestus, and grant me excellence and wealth.

XXI.

TO APOLLO.

Of Thee, O Phoebus, even the swan sings clearly with the music of its wings, leaping on the bank by the swirling river Peneius, and of Thee with his tuneful lyre the sweet-voiced minstrel ever singeth first and last.

Hail to thee, O King! I pray to thee in song.

XXII.

TO POSEIDON.

I begin to sing of Poseidon, mighty god of the sea, mover of earth and barren main, who is lord of Helicon and broad Aegae. Twofold is the honour, O Earth-shaker, which the gods have granted thee, to be Tamer of horses and Saviour of ships. Hail! Poseidon, dark-haired Girdler of Earth! Do thou, O Blessed God, with gracious heart, aid the mariner.

XXIII.

TO ZEUS.

I shall sing of Zeus, the best and greatest of the gods, Far-glancer, King, Fulfiller, who holdeth frequent converse with Themis as she reclineth on her seat.

Be gracious, O Far-glancing Son of Kronos, most glorious and most mighty!

XXIV.

TO HESTIA.

O Hestia! who guardest the sacred shrine of Apollo, the Far-darter, in holy Pytho, ever doth the soft olive oil drop from thy locks. Come to this house, graciously approach with Zeus the Counsellor, and grant also favour to my song.

XXV.

TO THE MUSES AND APOLLO.

I shall begin with the Muses, and Apollo, and Zeus. From the Muses and Far-darting Apollo are the minstrels and harpers upon earth, and from Zeus are kings. Blessed is the man whom the Muses love, sweetly from his mouth floweth his voice.

Hail! children of Zeus! Honour ye my song. And I shall remember you and another lay.

XXVI.

TO DIONYSUS.

I begin to sing of Ivy-crowned, boisterous Dionysus, noble son of Zeus and glorious Semelé, whom the fair-tressed Nymphs took to their bosoms from the king his father, and fed and reared him carefully in the dells of Nyssa. He waxed strong by the grace of his sire in a fragrant cave, being numbered among the immortals. Now when the goddesses had nurtured this famous god, he would wend down the woodland haunts, thick-garlanded with ivy and laurel. And the Nymphs attended him as he led the way. And their din filled the wide forest.

Hail to thee, O Dionysus of the Rich Clusters. Grant that again in joy we may reach the Time of Vintage.

XXVII.

TO ARTEMIS.

I sing of Clear-voiced Artemis of the Golden Distaff, Virgin Revered, Huntress of Stags, Delighter in arrows, own sister of Apollo of the Golden Sword, who over the shady fells and windy heights, in joyaunce of the chase, straineth her golden bow, loosing her whistling shafts. The tops of lofty mountains tremble, and wildly echoes the dusky forest to the cry of beasts; and the earth thrills, and the fish-teeming sea. And the goddess, brave of heart, hies hither and thither, destroying the race of beasts. But when the huntress, proud of her bow, is content, and hath gladdened her heart, she slackens her bent bow, and cometh to the great hall of her dear brother, Phoebus Apollo, in the rich land of Delphi, marshalling the fair band of Muses and Graces. Then hanging up the arching bow and arrows, with fair braveries about her, she leadeth them out and beginneth the dances. And they, lifting up their divine voices, sing of fair-ancled Leto, how she bore as children far the best of the gods in deeds and counsel.

Hail! Children of Zeus and fair-tressed Leto. I shall remember you and another lay.

XXVIII.

TO ATHENÉ.

I begin to sing of the famous goddess, Pallas Athené, Bright-eyed, Inventive, Stern-hearted, Virgin Revered, Valiant Protectress of cities, Tritogenia, whom Zeus the Counsellor himself brought forth from his august head in war-gear golden and bright. Wonder took hold of all the immortals when they saw it. Quickly did the goddess leap from the immortal head of Aegis-bearing Zeus, and stand before him shaking her sharp javelin. And mighty Olympus trembled terribly under the weight of the bright-eyed goddess; the earth around groaned sorely, the sea heaved in turmoil of purple waves, and the spray was suddenly belched forth.

The noble son of Hyperion stayed his fleet horses for a long time till the virgin Pallas Athené did the divine war-gear off her immortal shoulders. And Zeus the Counsellor smiled.

Hail to thee, Child of Aegis-bearing Zeus! I shall remember thee and another lay.

XXIX.

TO HESTIA.

O Hestia! Thou who hast gained an eternal home in the lofty dwellings both of immortal gods and of folk who fare below—the chiefest honour! Thou who receivest a fair and precious portion, for never are banquets of mortals held whereat the master of the feast doth not pour forth sweet wine to Hestia, first and last!

And Thou, O Slayer of Argos, Son of Zeus and Maia, Messenger of the Blessed, God of the Golden Wand, Giver of good things! be gracious, and with revered and beloved Hestia grant me aid. Ye twain haunt the fair homes of earth-born mortals; your hearts are kindly to each other, and are skilled in glorious deeds. Grant to me wisdom and youth.

Hail! Daughter of Cronos, and Thou, Hermes of the Golden Wand, I shall remember you and another lay.

XXX.

TO THE MOTHER OF ALL.

I shall sing of Gaia, Mother of All, Strong-founded, Most Ancient, who feedeth all things that are in the world, both things which move over the divine earth, and in the sea, and things which fly—these are all fed from her store.

By thee, Revered Goddess, are men rich in children and harvests, and thine it is to give life to mortals, and take it away. Blessed is the man whom thine heart shall delight to honour; all things in abundance hath he. His tillage is laden with fruitfulness, his fields abound in herds, and his house is filled with goods. They whom thou shalt honour, O August Goddess, Bountiful Deity, rule as lords with good laws in a city of fair women, and great riches and wealth attend them. Their children exult in fresh gladness, and their maidens with blithe hearts sport in flowery dances and skip over the soft blossoming lea.

Hail! Mother of the Gods, Wife of starry Uranos. In thy favour grant me in return for my song a pleasant life. And I shall remember thee and another strain.

XXXI.

TO HELIOS.

O Muse Calliope, begin now to sing of Helios, the Shining God, whom large-eyed Euryphaessa bore to the son of Gaia and starry Uranos. For Hyperion wedded famous Euryphaessa, his own sister, and she bore to him beautiful children, rosy-armed Eos, and fair-haired Selené, and unwearied Helios, peer of the immortals, who shineth for men and deathless gods when he hath mounted his steeds. Terrible is the glance of his eyes from under his golden helmet. Bright beams flash radiantly from him. On his head bright flaps at his temples guard his beautiful far-shining face. About his body flameth a fair and delicate garment. Fleeter far than the moving wind are his stallions,* when he driveth his golden chariot and his steeds, and speedeth them at evening through the sky to the ocean. Hail! O king, graciously vouchsafe sweet life. And beginning with thee, I shall celebrate the race of speech-gifted heroes, whose deeds the gods have revealed to men.

---

* xxxi. 14, 15. I prefer the reading supported by Hermann—
λεπτουργὲς πνοιῆς ἀνέμων πολὺ θάσσονες ἵπποι·
εὖτ' ἂν ὅγ' ἰθύσας, &c.

XXXII.

TO SELENÉ.

Ye Muses, skilled in song, tuneful daughters of Zeus, the Son of Cronos, sing of the fair-faced broad-winged Moon. The gleam from her immortal head, revealed in the sky, rolls round the earth, and much beauty ariseth under her burning light. The murky darkness is lighted up from her golden crown, and her beams flood the air, when divine Selené hath bathed her fair body in the ocean, and done on her far-shining robes, and yoking her strong-necked glossy colts driveth swiftly forward her rich-maned teamsters in the mid-month at eventide. Her great orbit is accomplishing, and her beams are brightest in the sky when she is waxing to the full. She is a mark and a sign for men.

With her once the Son of Cronos mingled in the couch of love, and she conceived and bare a daughter, Pandia, who was gifted with surpassing beauty among the gods.

Hail! O Queen, white-armed goddess, divine Selené, fair-haired and gracious! Beginning with thee I shall sing the praises of heroes, whose deeds minstrels, the henchmen of the Muses, celebrate with charming voices.

XXXIII.
TO THE DIOSCURI.

Ye quick-glancing Muses! sing of the Sons of Zeus, the Tyndaridae, glorious children of fair-ancled Leda—Horse-taming Castor and blameless Polydeuces. She brought them forth under the heights of the mighty hill Taygetus, after the love embraces of Dark-clouded Zeus—her sons the saviours of earth-born men and swift-faring ships, when wintry blasts rush over the pitiless sea.

The mariners in prayer invoke the sons of Mighty Zeus with white lambs, mounting their vessel's poop. The strong wind and the sea-waves drive the ship beneath the water. But suddenly the gods appear darting through the sky on tawny wing, and straightway they abate the blasts of vexing winds, and calm the waves on the white sea waters—a happy omen for the sailors, the ending of their toil. They are glad at the sight, and cease their weary labour.

Hail! ye Tyndaridae, riders of swift steeds, I shall remember you and another lay.

XXXIV.
FRAGMENTS OF A HYMN TO BACCHUS.

Some men say that in Dracanum, others in windy Icarus, others in Naxos, others by the deep-eddying river Alpheius, Semelé conceived and bare thee, Eiraphiotes, a divine son to Zeus, who delighteth in thunder. But some, O Prince, falsely aver that thou wert born in Thebes. Far from mortals did the Father of Gods and men beget thee, hiding from white-armed Hera. There is a certain Nyssa, a lofty mountain blooming with woods, far from Phoenicé, near the streams of Aegyptus.

. . . . . .

"And they will erect thee many a statue in thy temples. As these (exploits) are three, men will ever offer to thee perfect hecatombs every third year." Thus spake Zeus the Counsellor, and nodded with his head.

Be gracious, Eiraphiotes, frenzied Lover. We minstrels sing of thee when we begin and when we end. In no wise is it possible to forget thee and remember sacred song.

Hail to thee, Dionysus Eiraphiotes, and to thy mother Semelé, whom men call Thyoné.

FINIS.

www.ingramcontent.com/pod-product-compliance
Lightning Source LLC
Chambersburg PA
CBHW020126170426
43199CB00009B/651